"Jeff has a way of truly breaking you through the weaving of poetic wisdom and brutally honest truth. He has taken my breath away many a time with the depths in which his writing asks me to explore within my own being."

—LeAnn Rimes, actress, author, songwriter, Grammy Award-winning singer

"*Hearticulations* beats with organic wisdom, raw truth, and soulful love. Jeff skillfully reminds us not to bypass our messy, miraculous human experience and encourages us to dive deep into our body and our wounds so we can mine and share authentic gold. His poetic, hard-earned, no BS insights provide a much-needed weight within the modern spiritual arena and his heart provides a much-needed embrace."

—Sera Beak, author of *The Red Book, Red Hot and Holy: A Heretic's Love Story,* and *Redvelations: A Soul's Journey to Becoming Human*

"In *Hearticulations*, Jeff Brown guides the reader on a heartfelt path of living and loving consciously. This transformation begins and ends with embracing who we are and grounding in our divine purpose for being here.

These quotes and stories will support the reader to create the bridges our world needs now, to navigate the arising complexities and to love even greater in the midst of fear and uncertainty. This offering is a true gift."

—Carley Hauck, author of *Shine: Ignite your inner game to lead consciously at work and in the world,* Leadership Development Consultant, and Speaker

"*Hearticulations* is Jeff Brown's beautiful gift to a collective crying out for kindness and compassion. A deeply moving ensemble of words celebrating the healing and eternal power of love, reminding us once again that what matters most is love."

—Paul Samuel Dolman, author of *Hitchhiking with Larry David,* host of the *What Matters Most* podcast

"Your heart is whispering to you. Are you listening? Have you deciphered its murmurs and hushed tones? Jeff Brown's new book *Hearticulations* not only infuses us with inspiration but also guides the way for each of us to listen to and live from the heart."

—Jason Digges, author of *Conflict = Energy*

"Jeff Brown does it again, illuminating the illusions and realities of the path of awakening. Like a skilled martial artist, he probes, jabs and makes combination blows to the distortions and elevated fluffiness of spirituality. Each quote is a volume of wisdom ready to shake complacency and escapism into real useful awareness. If you want to save years of endless inner meanderings and spiritual distractions and go straight for the potent gems of Truth for real...then devour each sentence slowly and apply liberally."

—Satyen Raja, founder of *WarriorSage Trainings*

"Reading *Hearticulations* felt like I was sitting in front of a wise mentor who had turned his courageous adventures of spirit and heart into an illuminating guide helping others walk home towards themselves. There is a unique depth in Jeff's writing that speaks to the soulful and spiritual within us, while also acknowledging and touching the tender human within us too. *Hearticulations* is filled with incredibly deep and grounded knowledge and heart-full wisdom. It unpacks a variety of universal themes that often get spiritually bypassed or become misrepresented in mainstream pop psychology, such as boundaries, and anger, and masculinity. It is filled with wonderful teaching stories that empower, validate, and give us permission to embrace the tenderness of our human heart. What an absolute gem!"

—Silvy Khoucasian, relationship coach and creatress

Other Books by Jeff Brown

Soulshaping: A Journey of Self-Creation
Ascending with Both Feet on the Ground
Love It Forward
An Uncommon Bond
Spiritual Graffiti
Grounded Spirituality

HEARTICULATIONS

– On Love,
Friendship,
and Healing –

Jeff Brown

ENREALMENT PRESS
TORONTO, CANADA

Published by Enrealment Press
PO Box 65618,
Dundas, Ontario, Canada
L9H-6Y6

Cover photo by Grey Carnation/Shutterstock
Cover design by Susan Frybort
Book design by Allyson Woodrooffe
Printed in the USA

Library and Archives Canada Cataloguing in Publication

Title: Hearticulations /Jeff Brown.
Names: Brown, Jeff, 1962- author.
Identifiers: Canadiana (print) 20200272659 | Canadiana (ebook)
20200272667 | ISBN 9781988648057
   (softcover) | ISBN 9781988648064 (PDF)
Subjects: LCSH: Brown, Jeff, 1962-—Quotations. | LCSH: Love—
Quotations, maxims, etc. | LCSH:
   Interpersonal relations—Quotations, maxims, etc.
Classification: LCC PN6084.L6 B76 2020 | DDC 302.3—dc23

I dedicate this book to Canada, my beloved home. When I was young, I had no idea how blessed I was to be born in this great country. But now I do. And I am deeply grateful for this beautiful land and its heartfelt people. I could not have written these passages anywhere else.

HEARTICULATIONS

— On Love,
Friendship,
and Healing —

It's not about "letting it go." It's about letting it in. It's about letting it deep. It's about letting it through. It's about being true to your feelings. It's about giving your experiences the attention they deserve. And that may take a moment, or it may take years. The trick is not to shame your need to hold on to what has yet to be resolved. "Let it go" is the mantra of the self-avoidant, feigning resolution because they lack the courage or the preparedness to face their feelings. Let's not play that game. Let's let things in and through, until they are fully and truly ready to shift. Let's let it grow into the transformation at its heart. We write our story by fully living it. Not by "letting it go" before its time.

You are the sign you have been waiting for. It's not in the stars, nor is it at the heart of everything synchronistic. It's not stamped on the forehead of your beloved, nor is it lingering on the tip of the guru's tongue. It's not in the numerology, or the astrology, or floating on the wings of your angel-guides. It's already here. It's you. That you exist at all, with all the odds that were stacked against your incarnation, is evidence of your significance. So are all the gifts, callings, and offerings that course through your veins. You are a signpost of miracle and wonder. It serves the shaming powers-that-be if you look for your signs outside of yourself... but you won't find them there. You will find them in your own bones, right at the heart of your lived experience. After you clear the blinding clutter, you will realize that it was you all along. You are the sign that leads you home.

The glorification of busy will destroy us. Without space for healing, without time for reflection, without an opportunity to surrender, we risk a complete disconnect from the authentic self. We burn out on the fuels of willfulness, and eventually cannot find our way back to center. And when we lose contact with our core, we are ripe for the picking by the unconscious media and other market forces. After all, consumerism preys on the uncentered. The further we are from our intuitive knowing, the more easily manipulated we are. And the more likely we are to make decisions and affix to goals that don't serve our healing and transformation. To combat this, we have to form the conscious intention to prioritize our inner lives. To notice our breath, our bodies, our feelings. To step back from the fires of overwhelm and remember ourselves. It may feel counter-intuitive in a culture that is speed-addicted, but the slower we move, the faster we return home.

At some point on the journey, you may reach a point where you want to ease the throttle of transformation. Not where you stop growing, but where you stop utilizing your will to effect personal change. You're still growthful, but it's different. It's gentler, and more about accepting what is, than changing it. You reach a place where you are more embracing of who you are, and of how far you have come, and you feel ready to work with what you've got. It's important to notice this moment, if it arrives. Because there is a real peace in that tender self-acceptance. And, ironically, it may ignite the most profound change of all.

I grew up in a broken home. But not because my parents divorced. It was broken long before, when the love turned to hate. When they finally divorced, there was actually more room to breathe. All the energy that went into managing the breaks, could be channeled into healing. It's time we re-framed the shaming term, "broken home." It is riddled with assumption and judgement. And it neglects the fact that many single parents hold their families together beautifully. While many seemingly intact families, are deeply broken. Because a home is not broken when parents separate or divorce. A home is broken when there is an absence of love. If there is love, nothing's broken.

I have a particularly difficult time with "corrective listeners." These are the friends who listen to what you are going through, and then correct it. For example, you tell them how difficult things are right now, and they remind you of all the things you have accomplished. Or, you share your economic challenges, and they tell you all the ways you can make more money. Or, you share your grief around a personal loss, and they list off the names of those who are still in your life. Their intentions are often very positive and sincere, but what gets lost is the healing nature of simply being heard. Not improved upon—HEARD. This is the best way to improve each other's realities. Listening in.

It certainly feels good to imagine that the entire dysfunctional family will heal and mend. I held out for that vision of possibility for many years, largely because of the toxic, codependent nature of my trauma. If we suffered together, then we would rise together. But it seldom happens this way, both because of the complex nature of ancestral trauma, and because it takes so much energy and imagination to craft a healthier way of being. Most people who have been trapped beneath the rubble of family madness, don't have the energy, or the faith to get out from under it. It has become who they are. But you have to keep going. Traversing your path. You have to give yourself permission to shed the paradigm, even if it's lonely, even if you feel the temptation to go back and wait on the others. Family dynamics can be like quicksand—they may end up dragging you down with them. Stay firmly planted on your path. We need you. Because the whole world changes when one gets out. Because you are our best hope for a healthier tomorrow. I know it's difficult to get out alone, but you are never truly alone. You are raising the bar for all of us.

What if it's only a 'nervous breakdown' if you bottleneck and bury the emotions that are trying to come through you? That's what causes the breakdown—the resistance to what is, the stopping of the process before it has an opportunity to move toward realization and resolution. What if something beautiful is actually happening within you, something that wants to heal and move into full authenticity? What if this is not a nervous breakdown—but a nervous break-through—a profound emotional cleansing, a dissolution of the false structures that have ruled your life, a breaking through to a more authentic state of being?

"Your vibe attracts your tribe." Sounds good, right? But it's not always true, because sometimes your vibe also attracts sociopaths, lite-dimmers, and border-crossers that come to steal your light. If you needed that lesson, then I suppose it's okay to call them part of your tribe, but if you didn't, then it's fair to say that your vibe also attracted an abuser. I have known many who bought into this bouncy 'New Cage' quote and let the wrong people through the door. Perhaps a grounded re-frame would serve us: "Sometimes, your vibe attracts your tribe. Sometimes, your vibe attracts that which doesn't serve you. And sometimes your vibe has nothing to do with any of it. Sometimes, a predator walks in your direction just because (s)he wants to." Be wary of spiritual clichés posing as truth.

You can't bring your voice to the world without triggering others. You can't humanifest your gifts without igniting someone's jealousy. You can't find your light without pissing someone off. It comes with the territory.

The story doesn't change when we pretend it was all an illusion. The story doesn't change when we get addicted to transcendence and float above it. The story doesn't change when we feign forgiveness and resolution. The story doesn't change when we confuse dissociation with expansion. The story doesn't change when we tell ourselves that there are no victims. The story changes when we own our pain. The story changes when we work it through to the lessons at its core. The story changes when we are truly seen in our suffering. The story changes when we heal our heart. We are made of story—there's no shame in that. Either we work through our story, or our story will work through us.

As friendships grow closer, conflict becomes more difficult to avoid. And this is often a good thing. Because the closer we get to each other's hearts, the more triggers rise into view. Because you can't fully know someone until you ignite each other's ire. Because you won't know if a connection has legs, until it has been tested by conflict. And when it is, there is a choice to be made—walk away in disgust, or walk toward in an effort to deepen the connection. Conflict isn't the adversary of connection. Fear of confrontation... is.

I understand the need for answers about how another feels about us and why they behave the way they do. It is natural to want to make sense of things before deciding to either go in deeper, or cut the cord in a relationship. But I do not feel that we should put our lives on hold if those answers are not forthcoming. It may be that they do not have a clear answer, or perhaps they do not have the capacity to communicate their feelings. Or, perhaps they are hiding something. Whatever it is, waiting a long time for another to come clean is a big mistake. At some point, we need to bring the question home: Why am I putting my life on hold for another? Why am I giving this much power away? What beliefs about my own value are feeding into this holding pattern? If someone can't or won't communicate, it's truly their loss. We have a precious life to live. Onwards and upwards...

Depression is frozen feeling. It's not a disease of the 'mind.' It's a disease of the heart. It is sourced in unexpressed, unreleased, and unhealed pain that is held deep within the physical and emotional body. You can talk about it in therapy to soften its edges, you can medicate it in the hope that it becomes more manageable, but the real work has to happen somatically, deep within the body itself. The frozen material has to be thawed out, worked through, released. Our shadow is not our enemy. Repression is. Unfortunately, we still live in a world that is afraid of the source material. So we shun it, bury it, 'manage' it with dissociative spiritualities, medications and feelings-avoidant psychoanalysis. All of this merely perpetuates and concretizes the problem. The only way to heal depression is to get to its roots. To get right inside those frozen feelings, and thaw them out somatically. We felt the initial pain in our bodies. We must go right back inside of our bodies to feel and resolve it. No more damming up of our emotions. No more defenses and denials. THE FEEL IS FOR REAL. Let's feel our way back to life.

We are not just here together to keep each other company. We are here together, to show each other God. The portal is each other.

Perhaps we should stop calling our shadow, our trauma, our tender woundedness, and the consequent issues, 'our demons.' This feels like the kind of term that was used to manipulate us into believing we are all shameful sinners that must be controlled and contained. If I have a perpetual problem, it's a wound. Or it's a cry for healing. Or it's a nexus for transformation. But it's not a demon.

Dissolving the ego is an act of self-hatred. Because it is intrinsic to the self and essential for healthy human functioning. Don't rid yourself of ego. Strengthen its healthy aspects. Transform its unhealthy aspects. Ennoble it.

While I appreciate the value of speaking our truths in relationship about what triggers us, I also recognize the value of expressing our gratitudes. This is particularly essential for those with an abundance of unresolved and easily projected childhood material. The narcissistic nature of early wounding can often leave us in a state of perpetual trigger, making it difficult to move from compassion in our connection with loved ones. We share the negative stuff that comes up in the relationship, while forgetting to share our love, our respect, our appreciation, our deep regard for all that they overcome and offer on a daily basis. It has to be balanced, or defenses will be erected, and individual and relational progress will be stalled. In other words, for every bit of bratitude, offer an abundance of gratitude. We must never deny the beauty that someone brings.

We give away so much power to our birth parents, to define our value. In some cases, it works out just fine. They love, honor, and attune to us until we are ready to carry that nourishment forward in our own life. The perfect love hand-off. But all too often, they fail to plant the seed of self-love within us and we wander through our lives looking for it, often in the wrong places. Or worse, we keep going back to the same empty parental well, somehow imagining that it will one day nourish us with love. But it can't, not because we are unworthy, but because of their own limitations and unresolved issues. It took me years to accept that my parents were not the rightful determiners of my value. They were just the bodies that the divine chose to bring me here. My value, your value, is in our own two hands. Better we drink from our own sweet wells—divine waters overflowing at the banks—to recognize our value. The oceans of essence begin within, again and again…

What the world needs now is a true conversation. Not a conversation between our adaptations, disguises and defenses. Not a conversation that hides our truth under a bushel of shame. Not a conversation about what doesn't matter. But a conversation that is revealed, revealing, deeply genuine. Perhaps that is the key to most everything...true sharing from the deep within. Nothing to hide, nowhere to hide it...

As I get older, I am so acutely aware of how little time is left in this incarnation. Not in a negative sense, but in an in-powered sense. How to neglect sacred purpose when you really grok death? How to waste time walking false-path when you know your time is limited? Death consciousness becomes a glorious fuel for the fire of authenticity. Why wait until our deathbeds to awaken, when the opportunity stands before us in this very moment. No way of knowing how much time is left. Let's spend it doing all that we can to live true to path.

Real love is intense, but it's not dangerous. It's passionate, but not abusive. It's vulnerable, but not risky. Those who think love must feel dangerous, often grew up in homes where love was associated with destruction. There was love, but there was so much chaos attached to it that the two became internally indistinguishable. If so, our work now is to learn how to associate love with safety. Not a boring kind of safety, but the kind that is infused with genuine self-care. We set the stage for real love, when we learn how to love ourselves enough to protect ourselves from harm.

Many severe trauma survivors will never fully heal, let alone come to believe they were 'right where they were supposed to be' when the traumas occurred. Not everything is about 'the courage to heal.' Some people have been too deeply traumatized and simply cannot utilize their will in those ways. It takes all that they have, and more courage than many of us can imagine, just to keep going. Until we get that, I mean truly get that, we will not create the kind of compassionate world we all need.

Let there be no doubt: All love connections are not created equal. Some bonds are simply practical. Others are blindly rooted in pathology and old traumas. Still others are opportunities to heal and have essential needs finally met. And some have a mystical quality from the first meeting. Pure and simple. Apparent from the first out-breath. Unmistakably sacred. God rising on the wings of their love. This is how the timely and the timeless become indistinguishable—when Love meets God deep in the heart's inner temple.

As many of us have found out, silence can be violence when it is used in an effort to wound. It is one of the most potent ways to cause deep suffering. And it's a very effective strategy, particularly when utilized on highly relational beings. Because highly relational beings are built for dialogue. They are ready, willing, and able to process the material that comes up between them and those they are connected to. They don't know any other way. When they are denied that opportunity, they suffer. And not just on an emotional level—they suffer immunologically as well. They become more at risk of disease when the bridge to expression is blocked. Because all those unsaid words and unprocessed feelings congeal inside, weakening their physical well-being. If you are someone who is still carrying the remnants of unresolved material that was denied expression by silent treatment, do your best to move that material through you. If you can't do it with the silencing aggressor, do it with a therapist, or with another friend. Don't allow someone else's silence to imprison you in a museum of old pain. Express it fully, move it on through. It's not yours for the keeping.

When you grow up in a very imprisoning home environment, it is easy to conclude that the world will be equally as imprisoning. Because your childhood home was your whole world. If it wasn't safe, how could a world filled with strangers be safer? It's hard to imagine that the big world out there could actually be a warm and cozy place. And this generalization from our early life experience can easily become a self-fulfilling prophecy that keeps our suffering alive in our adult years. We continue to pick unsafe people and situations, either because this is all we know ("better the devil you know"), or because we don't believe in more life-affirming possibilities. Or, we commit to absolutely nothing real, because we associate all forms of commitment and attachment with imprisonment. We move through our lives imagining ourselves "free spirits," when all we really are is trauma survivors on the run from unresolved pain. When you were locked in with aggressors, escape was your only hope. But after they are gone, the real freedom comes from being able to commit to everything that serves you, and to know that you are safe in the heart of the world. That's real freedom, right there.

It's not all in your head. It's all in your heart. It's all in your feet. It's all in your hips. It's all in your shoulders. It's all in your breath. It's all in your body. Anything unattended to, unresolved, unhealed, and unprocessed lives in your tissues, your cells, your musculature. It may be manifest in your thinking, but it doesn't begin there. The mind does not source itself—the body does. The trick is to not try to shift your thinking from within the mind itself. You can't. You may be able to subdue it there, but you won't be able to resolve it. Because the troubling thoughts are merely a symptom of the deeper issues. They are a reflection of our emotional holdings and constricted musculature. They emanate from the fleshy trauma tunnels that we dug in order to survive this world. Many of us sit in the waiting room of awakening for decades, waiting impatiently for our new birth. Yet it never arrives, because we are looking for it where it isn't—within the mind, itself. Babies aren't born that way. You have to go down into the depths of the body to bring a new birth to life. Down, down, down... into the alchemical chambers of new thought—YOUR MAGNIFICENT BODY. This is where we are born again.

Healthy boundaries aren't walls or barbed wire fences. They are gates, portals that we selectively open when it is safe and life-enhancing to do so. Sometimes we do have to wall others off—to heal, to get a taste of what it feels like to be protected after a mountain of suffering— but eventually we come into a sacred balance. Here, we make conscious decisions as to when to open, when to close. I think of it as the "art of selective attachment." Rather than responding from a patterned place, that is too open or too closed, we assess each situation on its own merits. We keep the gate closed, when it is risky to open it. We unlatch the gate, if there is a healthy basis for connection. Healthy boundaries are situation specific, evolving and clarifying as we grow. We sift connections through an intelligently discerning filter, only opening the gate to those experiences and individuals that enhance our sacred true-path. Boundaries, boundaries, boundaries… don't leave home without them.

In our efforts to heal and integrate all that we are, it is essential that we learn to love our varied parts. To see how hard they have worked to adapt us, to protect us, to direct us, to keep us afloat. But it's not enough to merely love them. We also have to hear them. We have to give them voice, to hear precisely what they have to say about what they know. We have to hear what intrinsic wisdom they contain. They were birthed by wounding and circumstance, and they want to share their origins with us. They want us to understand why they vigilantly developed in an effort to save us. They want us to remember what we have been through together. Because the remembrance is what integrates us. Because the going back in time is what brings us into the moment. This is the nature of true inclusivity. Every aspect gets a seat at the table of presence, every voice gets heard, every part is woven into the wholly weave of selfhood. You want to live an inclusive life? Become one with all of your parts. They've all been essential to your survival. The best friends you will ever have.

The boundless loves can seldom be limited by space and time. But that's not why they come. They come for a different reason. To awaken, to enhearten, to crack through the armor that encases our tender woundedness. They are anything but gentle. They are the great wake-down call that shatters us into bits. We either lay on the ground in pieces, or we rise to the invitation and become a truer, more authentic form. No longer living a step back from the shore, we plummet heartlong into a sea of deep feeling. We live our life as love, swimming for evermore in the heart of its embrace. Yes, boundless love hurts, but it also births new forms.

People-pleasing is a self-protective pattern. If we keep them happy, they won't turn on us. But it comes at a terribly high price. Because in our fixation with keeping others happy, we undermine our own happiness. In our desire to placate others, we deny ourselves. Perhaps it's time for a new way: Please others, when it truly pleases you.

Sexual assault against women is an epidemic of epic proportions. More than half of the women I know well, have been assaulted in one form or another. If any other form of dysfunction impacted that many people, we would declare a state of emergency. It is perhaps the most socially acceptable epidemic on this planet. And it has to stop. Women can no longer live with these secrets, nor can they walk this earth fearful of where they step. But they cannot do it alone. Awakening men must join them. We must stand firmly beside them, and stand down those unconscious men who frighten and assault our sisters. We must make a conscious choice not to shun women, but to shun those men who belittle and abuse them. This is the next step, one that I believe holds the key to world transformation. Because if half the planet is denied basic protections, the entire planet is lost. May recent events be a true, never-to-be-forgotten call to action for awakening men everywhere. Courageously confront and transform the aggressor that lives within you. Give him no place to hide. It is not shameful to acknowledge your violent conditioning. It is shameful to act upon it. Make another choice. Stand beside your sisters. Stand down your unconscious brothers. Stand for something humane. Make love your lasting legacy.

It took me years to understand that many of us are more afraid of happiness than misery. Because misery and martyrdom have an inherent safety about them— one is never particularly vulnerable, nor at risk of disappointment. Unhappiness becomes a security blanket, a way to armor ourselves against deep feeling. On the other hand, happiness has an intrinsically risky quality. When we open our hearts to life, we are always vulnerable to loss, to shattering, to having it all fall away. But it can also expand and deepen, joyfully permeating every element of our life. I can often sense when someone has made unhappiness their shield, their perpetual life stance. Locking ourselves into a negative way of being is a self-fulfilling prophecy: misery begets misery. Only through risking something can we arrive at a new perspective. And most significantly, because the rhythms and tides of one's life can truly shift in the blink of an eye. All it takes is one good day and the whole damn thing can come back to light...

You hide from yourself when you hide from relationship. That's not to say that we don't need a break at times, but there is a price paid for too much social distancing. I spent a lot of time alone, certain of my self-actualization. And then human connections reminded me that there were many roads left to travel. Because intimacy with others makes us more intimate with ourselves. Because we are fundamentally relational beings, and we remain blind to many of our issues-in-need-of-healing when we avoid human contact. Alone, we can only travel so far on the trailways of transformation. Together, lots of grist for the soul mill. After we develop a strong foundation of selfhood, we need relational co-creation to invite us to the next stage of awakening.

It's not about someone stealing our heart. It's about restoring its aliveness. It's about softening its armor. It's about filling it up with light. When real love enters, it doesn't take anything from us. It gifts us with the everything.

Please love yourself. I am so very tired of this traveling ancestral shame show. So many of us wandering around not happy with who we are, not comfortable in our own skin, swearing we will finally celebrate our lives when we finally do that one next thing. When does it end? It ends when we end it. It ends when we clear the emotional debris and try a self-celebratory way of being on for size. Not when someone's love for us hands us back our self-worth, but when we embrace our worth on our own terms. Many of us go through our whole lives not loving ourselves for one minute. This has to stop. Let's stop it. Let's practice self-love. A little more every day. Please love yourself. You are so fucking divine.

Healing it is not about them changing. It's about you changing. If you wait for them to transform, you may be waiting for all eternity. If you focus on your own healing, the door to transformation opens.

Kudos to those parents who refuse to unfairly badmouth their ex-partners to their children, after the relationship ends. I feel that this choice is essential if you care about your children's well-being. They are entitled to make their own decision about their parent, based on their own direct experience, and they don't need to be unduly influenced by personal bias. It's one thing to share facts that they truly must know for their own protection—it's quite another to use the kid(s) as a dumping ground. My mother badmouthed my father for decades, both before and after they divorced, and it only caused more suffering and confusion. The fact is that he was half of us, and turning us against him was like turning us against ourselves. It was already difficult enough to deal with their divorce—we didn't need to divorce a part of ourselves as well. Those who can put a boundary around their anger at their ex, and continue to honor their children's right to love them, are making this world a much healthier place.

We will continue to project our stuff outside, until we work it through inside. We will continue to see the aggressor 'out there,' until we find out where he lives 'in there.' We will continue to fear authority, until we find our own inner authority. If you think your lens on reality isn't shaped by your unresolved material, you are mistaken. We will live life as projection, until we live life as truth. You want to see things as they are? First you have to see yourself, as you are.

Forget praying for world peace. Take to the streets and connect with lonely humans, feed the homeless, hug the world. Meditation In Action! That's a much more effective way to co-create world peace. I think of meditators I have known who gather together for two years to pray for the happiness of humanity while their fellow humans stand right outside the temple, needing a meal. Enough of these detached, emotionally safe versions of connectiveness. Better to spend five minutes feeding a homeless person than two years in meditation. Who doesn't need a hug?

It has to end, you know. The self-hatred. The collective shaming. The disdain for other. The emotional armor. The buried pain. The displaced humans. The misplaced kindness. The repressed trauma. The fake positivity. The meaningless materialism. The forgotten heart.

It has to begin, you know. The self-love. The collective healing. The love for other. The emotional release. The liberated pain. The welcomed humans. The perpetual kindness. The honored story. The authentic feeling. The meaningful purpose. The open heart.

It's time.

I call them, "the harborers." They are the people you connect with that always seem to be harboring animosity towards you. They don't outright say it, or create a space for relational resolution. Instead, they reveal it in various indirect forms: passive aggressive comments, a constant need to contradict you, a smile with a sinister energy coming off it. You can't put your finger on it, but you can just sense that they have an issue with you. They get under your skin, gnaw at you, leave you confused as to what is really going on. And that's precisely what they want you to feel. Because they don't actually have the courage to admit what they are feeling. And they want you to suffer for their avoidance. It's been my experience that it's best to rid your world of them. The fewer harborers, the better. Life is difficult enough, without confusing dynamics muddying the waters. Only clear communicators need apply.

Building a healthy self-concept takes more than recognizing why we don't have one. We have to do the work to actually construct a new egoic foundation. That work is not merely conceptual—it is rooted in embodied, lived experience: supportive relationships, positive affirmations coupled with meaningful action, addressing our emotional wounds, and eventually healing our way home. If you can stay with these tools for long enough, the voices of internalized shame and self-hatred will grow quieter, and a voice of self-love will rise up to occupy space inside of you. Your internal narrative will shift from one that is predicated on shame, to one that is predicated on a sense of your own value. You will no longer make choices sourced in an over-compensatory quest for external validation, you will make choices that are rooted in self-love. Self-regard will become your natural and organic way of being, and you will become emblazoned on your path, living your life like the force of purposeful nature that you are.

Blood is thicker than water. Yet it's also more likely to clot and destroy its hosts. There are two ways to understand family. One is through the survivalist lens: family are the ones you were born to. You bond together through thick and thin. You endure each other. You have each other's backs. You don't fall too far from the tree. If necessary, you hold yourself back so as not to leave anyone behind. The other idea of family is rooted in a more authentic perspective: family are those that reflect where you are at on your journey. People of *soulnificance* ("soul-family"), you bond together on the basis of shared resonance. You uplift each other. You support each other in becoming all that you are meant to become. You have no agenda for each other, beyond celebrating one another's uniquely unfolding sacred purpose. Two different ideas of family, two different worlds of possibility. Love, not blood. Survive, or thrive. Cling together for dear life, or invite each other to truly LIVE...

It's not about giving up on the fairy tale relationship. It's about landing it in reality. It's about giving the fairy feet. It's about peeling away the prince's armor and loving the real being down below. It's about wiping off the princess' makeup and loving her divine humanness. It's about finding romance in the naked fires of daily life. When our masks and disguises fall away, real love can reveal itself. Forget fairy tales, the human tale is much more satisfying. We just have to learn how to get turned on by humanness.

Don't brand yourself. Enreal yourself.

Unconditional love is a beautiful thing, as long as we don't use it against ourselves. I can love all of humanity, but that doesn't mean that I need to put up with all of humanity. The boundary, for me, is set at healthy self-regard. When my unconditional love for another undermines my self-respect, the fence goes up. Not because I don't believe in their possibilities, but because I have come to realize that there is no value in sacrificing my actuality for their potentiality. I make a distinction between human potential—which may well be infinite; and human actuality—which is often quite finite, particularly in those who choose, over decades, to remain asleep. Yes, they may eventually awaken, but we should never postpone any part of our own life waiting for that to happen. We should never hold back our own potential. Unconditional love begins at home, with the protecting and honoring of our own unique journey.

It is hard, these steps. Releasing the emotional debris that encases our heart. Shedding the false-identifications that obstruct our path. Shifting from survivalism to authenticity as a way of being. Bidding farewell to that which doesn't serve. It is hard, these steps. Because you are not just clearing your individual debris—you are releasing the debris carried by your entire ancestry. You are shedding the armor of millions before. You are saying goodbye to ways of being that have imprisoned countless generations. You are making the shift from a barbaric way of being to one that is genuinely human. Do not underestimate your significance, fellow seekers of the heart. We may be the first deep-release travelers. We may be the first authenticity-questing collective. We may be the first soulpod to consider the possibility that there is a sacred purpose at the heart of every birth. Our load, heavy. Our courage, essential. Our significance, profound. Our need for one another, irrefutable. We rise in unison, or not at all. We rise in unison, one hard-ass step after another...

It's not a pity party. It's pain. Stop dismissing it.

Emotional maturity and spiritual maturity
are synonymous.

We can't meet someone where they haven't met themselves. We may want to, but wanting doesn't make it so. Everyone's on their own unique journey. You can't push them to catch up with you. It just doesn't work like that. If they try, something will get broken or lost along the way. And they will actually end up further away from you than before. Better to honor their steps, just like you want others to honor yours. If you can't meet at the same place, bow to them and walk on. Do not guilt or shame them for being where they are. Respect it. It's their path to walk.

You are beautifully enough. Your stories of 'not good enough' are fictional novels written by a culture still hiding its light under a bushel of shame. The REAL story, your TRUE autobiography, is one of inherent magnificence, courage, and divinity flowing through your soul-veins. So you decide which book to read—the fictional novel written by those who do not SEE you, or the HOLY BOOK written by your glorious spirit.

One of the important things I learned after escaping my childhood home was that no one was entitled to steal my peace of mind. I didn't understand this when I was young. Throughout my childhood, I would watch as my good moods were continually undermined by the bad moods of others. If they weren't angry and blaming, they were depressed and despondent. There was no boundary anywhere, and no guidance on how to sustain genuine positivity in the heart of misery. Misery begot misery begot misery. It took many years to learn that there was another way of being in this world—one where I was allowed to protect my precious peace. And it was perhaps the most important lesson I ever learned at the School of Heart Knocks. Because if you allow yourself to get too close to lite-dimmers and border-crossers, you will deny yourself the life that awaits you. You will live under someone else's cloud until it becomes your own. Simply put, people are entitled to their moods, but they aren't entitled to yours. Your peace is not negotiable.

You can't measure your success by the number of people who follow you. You measure it by how true you are to path. Because if you aren't true to path, no amount of societal success will ever gratify you. And if you are true to path, the way that the world receives you is of little significance. Because you have already found your way home.

I am firmly of the view that this societal fixation on forgiving others is just another way that we bypass our own rightful anger, confusion, sense of loss. It is also a way that victims end up feeling blamed for their experience. I do agree that we can't forgive another until we self-honor, and that forgiveness is welcome if it's organic, but I also believe that forgiveness may have no place in certain dynamics. And that's entirely okay. Forgiveness is not a measure of our emotional health and well-being. Resolution is. That is, how we come to a relatively resolved understanding of what we went through, how we come to terms with what it was, in a way that brings us to a deeper understanding and peace... Resolution of process, is where it's at. And there is no reason to feel guilty if forgiveness does not arise within it. It's enough to find peace in the aftermath.

What makes a childhood perfect is not the conditions of our home environment, but how we converted its inherent imperfections into the fires of transformation. I have known many who claimed that they had perfect childhoods and entered adulthood dulled and uninspired, ill-prepared for life's challenges. And I have met many who endured horrifying childhoods, and entered adulthood passionate about living and ready to take on the world. What one person calls perfect, another calls hopelessly mediocre. What one person calls tragic, another calls preparation for a remarkable life. Perfect doesn't mean anything, if it doesn't set the stage for inspired action and a self-actualizing consciousness.

I long to find a way for all of us, to walk in each other's shoes for a few moments. To get right inside each other's experiences, perspectives, ancestral imprints. To empathically experience each other's circumstances, memories, unmet needs, delights. To break through the isolated nature of each person's framework of perception and to know it as our own. Imagine that world. Imagine what would happen next. We would stop seeing each other as threats and foreigners. We would recognize that we are all struggling to make sense of this life. We would recognize our shared humanity. We would begin to build bridges where before there were battlegrounds. I long to find a way for all of us, to walk in each other's shoes for a few moments. It would change everything.

I don't know of too many love connections that got anywhere good, when one had to 'fight' for the other. If you are fighting for love, lay down your arms and surrender. Because love meets us halfway, or nowhere at all. They will come if they wish, when they wish. And you will decide then how you feel about them. In the meantime, love yourself in every way possible.

When people tell you that you are being judgmental, they are judging you. And they usually tell you that when they don't like your opinion. When they like your opinion, they call it "wisdom" and "common sense." Funny how that works.

It's one thing to find your 'center' while detaching from the world. It's a whole other thing to find it at the heart of the world. For years, I left the world to find my 'self.' This was an essential step, because I was not yet self-connected enough to find my center in the heart of society. I was too light, too soft, too traumatized. But then I came to realize that if I couldn't hold to my center in the world, then I didn't have much of a center. If all it took was a few days in the marketplace, on urban streets, dealing with humanity, before I had to run back to the woods to find myself… then what had I found? A very fragile, hollow center. So the work continued, this time in the world itself. No easy feat, because of my trauma history, but the truest work I have ever done. Because now I can sit in the middle of hell, and feel my core. Because now I can stand amid the fires of distraction, and sustain my focus. It's one thing to find your center while hiding from the world. It's quite another to find it in the heart of the everything. Because the wholly grail is YOU, unstoppably solid in the heart of the madness.

You can connect from all kinds of places—energetic harmony, sexual alchemy, intellectual alignment—but they won't sustain love over a lifetime. You need a thread that goes deeper, that moves below and beyond the shifting sands of compatibility. That thread is fascination—a genuine fascination with someone's inner world, with the way they organize reality, with the way they hearticulate their feelings, with the unfathomable and bottomless depths of their being. To hear their soul cry out to you again and again, and to never lose interest in what it is trying to convey. If there is that, then there will still be love when the body sickens, when the sexuality fades, when the perfection projection is long shattered. If there is that, you will swim in love's waters until the very last breath.

You don't get cool hanging around 'cool people.' You don't get cool sitting before cool teachers. You don't get cool when you live in a cool town. You don't get cool when you sleep with cool people. You get cool when you go deeper into your own individuation. You get cool when you actualize your particular uniqueness. You get cool when you don't give a shit about being cool. Because what is cool is not an external reflection. It's not the chasing of cool. It's the surrender to your brilliance. It's the embodying of your own remarkable self. It's the development of your idiosyncratic voice. And it's the not caring one iota what others think about you because you are so deeply 'you' that external judgments are meaningless. You want to be cool? Be fully who YOU are. Authenticity is where it's at. Now, that's cool.

When people ask me how long it is going to take to heal all their wounds, I always respond the same way: "It's going to take a lifetime." This is seldom what they want to hear, particularly in this fast-paced and over-stimulated culture—but it's the truth. The emotional healing journey is a lifelong process, particularly for trauma survivors. Because trauma is not a concept. It's not a 'victim story' or a needless cry for attention. It's not something to 'rise above' or rush beyond with pseudo-positivity practices. Trauma is a lived, visceral experience, embedded in our emotional and physical bodies, that continues to interface with our consciousness throughout our lives. There is work that we can do to understand and transform our relationship with it, but it will continue to influence our experience of reality. And that's not necessarily a bad thing. Because it is fundamental to who we are. Because it's part of our real-time story, and at its heart are the seeds of our individual and collective transformation. How many great healers and world-changing activists did not endure tremendous suffering? Very few. Trauma is a door-opener to greatness. It's a portal to awakening. Let's not pretend it isn't there. Let's not deny its brazen wisdom. Let's roar it loud and true.

Friends fell away as I individuated on my soul's journey. As I shed one self-sense, I no longer identified with the people attached to it. Old ways of interacting seemed artificial, scripted, silly. Whereas before it was fine to hang out and waste time, now there was no time to lose. Now I had to protect my sacred purpose from connections that undermined it.

Be prepared for the lonely times on the journey. It can be very isolating to quest for true-path amid the trumpets of modern life. Walking through uncharted territory often means walking alone. This is particularly true in the transition stages before we find our consciousness soulpod. It's like primary school all over again—who will be my first REAL friends?

Intimacy is an informant. Not the kind of informant that shares inappropriate information, but the kind that tells us exactly what we need to know. If we allow ourselves to listen close, it whispers everything we are hiding from ourselves and each other. It shines a bright light on our unresolved shadow, exposing all the layers of armor that prevent us from being truly present with each other. Intimacy is surely 'in-to-me-see,' but it is also the only way to uncover the obstructions to true connection. Because we can only connect with another to the depths that we connect with ourselves. If we are a step back from our own hearts, we will always be a step back from everyone else's, too.

I call it "splintering." It's when intense stress or pressure re-triggers the emotional issues that you have worked through. It's those moments when an old pattern begins to show its challenging face again, long after you thought it resolved. This can be discouraging, feeling as though we have not made any progress. But we have. It's just the nature of our most stubborn stuff. We can work it through so effectively that we seldom see it under normal circumstances, but certain stresses or pressures can splinter our consciousness, and it rises up through the cracks, sometimes with a vengeance. When this happens, do not punish yourself or make the mistake of thinking that you have gone backwards. Instead, focus on what you can do to alleviate the stresses and bring yourself back into integration. Take action steps to bring your consciousness back into a cohesive form. If there is nothing you can do at the time, know that the issue will fade as soon as the strain subsides. This too will pass. And give yourself credit for how far you have come. The measure of transformation is not the complete eradication of our issues and patterns. The measure of transformation is how seldom they appear.

It's the greatest act of self-love to tend to your wounds and injuries. Your loving intention is an ointment that goes straight to the heart of the trauma, and sets your healing in motion. And it does something else. It sends the message to your wounded inner child that (s)he has value. That (s)he is worthy of attention. An echo of essence reverberates in the deep within, reminding you that YOU MATTER. When you repress your wounds, you validate your own insignificance. When you excavate and honor them, you empower your self-worth. You show yourself that you are worthy of love. You stand a little taller. HEALING IS THE BREAKFAST OF CHAMPIONS. It nourishes your body and soul, boosts your self-concept, and strengthens your resolve.

For those who love deeply, it can be perplexing when others turn away. But not everyone is ready to keep their heart-gate open to other humans. Not everyone can handle the vulnerabilities and risks. Some prefer substitute forms of love to the real thing. Perhaps they find it safer to channel their love toward a theoretical God that can never really hurt them, to a pet that will love them unconditionally, to a job that will gratify them economically without inspiring their passions. There are so many substitute gratifications on this planet, most of them a covering over of our deep longing to connect with each other. If you are one who is truly ready to love, better to attach to those who can meet you there. There is the love-lit world of genuine vulnerability, and the love-starved world of seeming security. Pick your path.

Fuck heightened consciousness—we aren't birds. Fuck transcendence-addiction masquerading as evolution. Fuck 'non-duality' that conveniently removes everything uncomfortable from the unified field. Fuck 'enlightenment' without integrity. Fuck patriarchal detachment models presented as 'the' royal road to the 'Kingdom' of God—what about the Queendom—our only hope. Fuck "The New Earth" as described by dissociative and disembodied pain bypassers. Fuck the yoga 'industry' that feigns awareness it does not hold. Fuck vertical spirituality that ignores what is happening before our very eyes. Fuck the bullshit soulebrities who don't give a shit about humanity. Fuck the guru who imagines himself realized. Fuck the New Cage movement and its trail of lies. Fuck any version of spirituality that doesn't SERVE humanity. Fuck the story bashers. Fuck the victim bashers. Fuck the bloodied spiritual lie. Embrace enrealment—before it's too fucking late.

We all want to actualize our callings, but timing is everything. I learned this the hard way. I always knew I would write, but I didn't understand that I needed to build the foundation first. So, I sat down to write, time and again, and I couldn't quite find my voice. I knew there was a writer living in there somewhere, but I couldn't find him. I needed a little more time, a little more suffering, a lot more lessons. I hadn't lived enough to manifest him.

In this driven world, we are often pushed to manifest too early. We are shamed for our uncertainty, insulted for our confusion, called lazy and selfish. But some callings need time to be cultivated. Some gifts cannot be opened too quickly. We have to craft them first, over time, in the fires of lived experience.

If you have a calling living inside of you, don't rush to manifest it. Trust your own instincts as to each step you need to take. Build the inner foundation you will need to see it through. Better to offer this ailing world one remarkable thing, than a hundred fragments of possibility. We need what you have to offer desperately.

Because many of us grew up with anxious attachments, we have a tendency to magnetize more of them in our adult lives. We do this out of habit, often because we have a fantastical (albeit unconscious) hope that we will finally heal this wound this way. It seldom works, because those who make us anxious seldom become those who make us secure. Anxious attachments can include partners that abandon, friends that flee when challenged, business arrangements that lack a solid commitment. Although our tendency is to replicate what we are used to, our best chance for healing this pattern is to learn how to magnetize secure attachments. Because if we keep connecting with those who are not capable of secure footing, we will keep sliding away from the life we long for. Where there is relational insecurity, there is no ground to support our personal expansion. It's like trying to build in the heart of an earthquake. Where there is relational security, there is a stable foundation for growth. With your feet solidly rooted, you can construct the life you deserve.

Some relationships have to end ugly. It's not the way we want it to be, but sometimes it's the way it has to be. Sometimes there is no possibility of a kind farewell. There is too much water under the bridge, or one or both parties are incapable of resolution, or it's just one of those woundmate connections that is riddled with unfriendly fire. Whatever it is, don't beat yourself up if an ending gets ugly. Don't pile more suffering onto the open wound. Difficult endings are part of life. They just are. Instead, focus your energies on learning what you need to learn so you can manifest something healthier the next time. Our lives don't improve when we expect perfection. They improve when we graduate from the School of Heart Knocks, one lesson after another... after another.

I cannot overemphasize the importance of working with a competent, grounded, and professional psychotherapist if you are wanting to process and heal deeply embedded issues and traumas. This is absolutely essential and should be put in place before you endeavor to put yourself in the hands of many, if not most, self-proclaimed 'spiritual healers.' There are many people in the 'spiritual' community who are passing themselves off as masters and shamans, yet they do not have the roots, or the solidity, or the egoic capacity to hold seekers safe. They are often individuals who have an economic, and/or egoic need to be seen in a particular light (in an effort to escape their own shadow), and they are not qualified to work with deep trauma. The very moment someone calls themselves a 'master,' you immediately know that they are full of shit. Because if they are that certain of their 'mastery,' they lack the humble capacity required to hold the space for another's material, and they will not have the wisdom to know when it's appropriate to refer someone out.

You don't have to apologize for how you feel. If you want to examine where those feelings come from, that's up to you. But don't do it because someone shames or guilts you for how you feel. That's their issue—not yours. We live in a world where how we feel is dismissed, re-framed, and manipulated at every turn. We must stand firmly in the truth of our feelings. Only from this place can we live an authentic life. Only from this place can we glow and grow.

Intensity is often confused with intimacy, particularly among those of us who grew up in extreme, unboundaried environments. Intensity becomes our idea of truly living, while more subtle and deeply present ways of relating get lost in the shuffle. If all we knew is intensity, it is easy to see stillness and attunement as boring, deadened ways of being. But this isn't necessarily the case. Sometimes they are the only way in, the great door-opener to in-to-me-see, the perfect conditions for bridging two hearts. If we can't connect when it is peaceful, we have to wonder if we are connecting at all. Intensity is not always what it's revved up to be.

Perhaps we can ask each other more questions. Real questions. The kind that connect us. Perhaps we can encounter each other from a place of honest inquiry and genuine curiosity—not assumption, not psycho-analytic categorization, not the egoic need to judge. Real inquiry. Here I am. Here you are. Curious about each other. Wondering how we got here. Allowing time to hear each other's stories. And to really listen. To get to know. To wonder. Inquiry changes everything.

When we are young, it's the illusion of perfection that we fall in love with. But as we age, it's the humanness that we fall in love with: the poignant stories of overcoming, the depthful vulnerability of aging, the struggles that grew us in karmic stature, the way a soul shaped itself to accommodate its circumstances. With less energy to hold up our armor, we are revealed, and in the revealing, we call out to each other's hearts. Where before wounds turned us off, they are now revealed as proof that God exists. Where we once saw imperfect scars, we now see evidence of a life fully lived.

It's been my experience that the person that families label the "crazy one" is often the sane one. This is particularly true in very dysfunctional families where ideas of healthy relating are turned upside down. These families often repress their authentic expression, and turn against any member who reminds them of their unresolved issues and patterns. As a result, the truth-speakers, the ones who refuse to contain their feelings, those who challenge the toxic status quo, are often scapegoated and vilified, made to feel crazy by those who lack the courage and insight to move beyond the family's madness. If you have been labeled the "crazy one," take heart. You are truly not alone. Most great creators and paradigm-shifters were met with fiery resistance by those afraid to grow. Whatever you do, do not allow your voice to be drowned out in the face of their judgments. Your voice, your vision, your ways of being, live at the heart of your unique soul's journey and are the key to collective transformation. No one has the right to bury them under a bushel of shame. No one! And remember, what is crazy to an unconscious person is often brilliantly sane to one who is awakening. Without people like you, the world is lost. Blessed be the "crazy ones!"

"Twin flames" is one of the most dangerous, delusional terms in the spiritual world. It reflects an ungrounded tendency, and often attracts New Cagers with very poor boundaries, who desperately want to believe that their unhealthy relationship is soul-sponsored. Maybe it is, but that doesn't mean it is healthy or sustainable. The moment someone says they are in a "twin flame" relationship I suggest that they buy a fire extinguisher and a burn kit. Because they are going to need them. What we need now are soul connections that are centered, grounded, sustainable, mature. Love has feet that walk it through time.

I have known many people who keep going back to the same empty well, sharing their truths and waiting for a certain response to liberate them. Waste of time—some people will never hear us or own their actions. We have to fill our own wells, but first we have to empty them of what isn't ours.

Empathy is an interesting word, often mistaken for something quite different—unhealthy boundaries, not knowing where we end and the other begins. I think of how often I remained connected to hurtful people (and others to me, when I was hurtful), because I imagined myself empathic. And maybe I was—but that didn't mean I had to endure their madness. Our empathic capacity can be as misdirected as any other ability. Just because you can feel where someone is coming from, doesn't mean that you have to put your emotional health at risk. When we allow 'empathy' to keep us invested in that which brings us suffering, when we confuse it with a boundaryless way of being, it morphs into misplaced faith and self-sabotage. It becomes compassion run amok. It turns a gift freely given, into a gift freely abused. Better to not turn your compassionate nature against yourself. Empathize with humanity, but shield yourself from harm.

I prefer the term "emotional illness" to mental illness. It may be true that our emotional material is often manifested in our thinking, but I also believe that the mind is not the primary source-spring for many conditions. The focus on the mental keeps us looking in the mind for the core issues, when so often the real issue lies within the emotional body, and requires more embodied, therapeutic approaches. Once someone is labeled "mentally ill," they often end up with an analytically-based psychiatrist who medicates them, rather than with a psychotherapist who can support their deeper healing. It feels very similar to the spiritual and patriarchal emphasis on the "monkey mind" as opposed to the "monkey heart." By focusing on the mind alone, we get trapped in a head-tripping loop and it becomes very difficult to liberate our consciousness. If we focus, instead, on healing the emotional material that sources the condition, there is hope for real change.

Out with the old, in with the true.

"Don't judge!" Yet in truth, we are judging all the time. We were granted the gift of discernment and critical thinking. Thank Goodness for that—it keeps us from walking down the wrong paths, making unhealthy decisions, destroying our lives. Even those who criticize judgment are judging. It's fundamental to the human experience. Perhaps the real question is not IF we are judging (or discerning, if you prefer), but WHY are we judging? Is it benevolently or malevolently intended? Are we judging in a forward-moving effort to distinguish unhealthy from healthy, or are we judging as a reflection of an unresolved superiority complex? Are we judging because we have a need to call out the madness of the world, or as a direct reflection of it? Where are we coming FROM?

We often pick partners that reflect our unresolved issues with our parents. Sometimes this works out well, particularly when both partners choose to consciously work through the material and grow together. But sometimes, it's an absolutely impossible dream-team, because the same characteristics that made the parent-child dynamic impossible are still present. The idea that we can shift ourselves or the other to finally make that kind of dynamic fruitful is simply untrue. Sometimes it is what it is, and our best chance of a healthy love relationship is to pick someone completely unlike the impossible parent. The therapeutic movement has to be careful to not make the assumption that every trigger-filled relationship is worthy of our time. Just because stuff comes up to work with, doesn't mean that it's worthy of our time. Stuff will come up in healthier connections too, but that stuff carries a seed of hope.

Those who have suffered the most will be our greatest teachers. Our lives have been so artificial for so long, that we need the trauma-speakers to save us. Because they are the closest to the truth of all of our lives. Because they are the most connected to the feelings that we are all burying—the individual cries for relief, the ancestral unresolveds that thread through each generation. It may seem counter-intuitive in this conditioned world, but those who have the courage to own their pain, are actually the ones we need the most. So next time you feel tempted to turn away from someone who wants to share their horribly painful story, stop. Just stop. Ask yourself why you are so eager to go—are they reminding you of something you don't want to feel within yourself? Then listen closely to them, and let them whisper your heart back to life.

Let's keep it grounded. EVERYTHING is not a gift. There may be valuable transformation that arises from many experiences, but that doesn't mean that EVERY experience is a gift. If we lean too far in that direction, we will deny trauma and victimhood altogether, a mechanism we have been employing for centuries. Some experiences are horrors, and it is all we can do to heal from them. To suggest that someone MUST find the gift in them, is to add insult to injury. It is also to create a culture that welcomes all forms of abuse, because, after all, "everything is a gift." Let's keep it real. Sometimes it's a gift. Sometimes it's a horror. And the only one who can decide that is the person who had the experience.

It's important to meet people where they are, not where we want them to be. There is a tendency, in many, to re-characterize people's experiences without being asked. You tell them you are feeling bad, they tell you all the reasons you should feel good. You tell them you are challenged by your circumstances, they tell you the way you can make things easier. You tell them that you have a plan to do something, they offer up another plan for you. There is a place for these offerings—particularly when requested—but often times they just make things worse. In fact, we are more likely to arrive at the next best place on our journeys when someone actually attunes to where we are, without making any effort to improve upon or re-frame it. We don't need to be saved—we need to be seen. That's the healing, right there. I hear you, I see you, I honor your choices... goes a long, long way.

Real intimacy is a meeting between two souls, an invitation to meet each other exactly where they are, without expectation or agenda. It doesn't demand gifts and benefits, sexual prowess, conditional offerings. It merely asks you to show up as you are, fully revealed and present. It invites you to shed your masks and disguises, to surrender to whatever is real for you in the moment. Real intimacy meets you right where you live, not where you or anyone else wants you to live. It's the big sigh of relief that arises when you finally know that you don't have to put on a show to feel seen or accepted. Here we are, just as we are. Hello.

There are people that you will never win with, no matter what you do. I call them "The Impossibles." The ones that always leave you feeling bad about yourself. I have known many. Often members of our own family, they are both the ones that we must avoid, and the ones that are the most difficult to avoid. If we continue to make an effort to connect, we are left feeling terrible about ourselves. If we disconnect altogether, we are left feeling guilty, selfish, perhaps responsible for their isolation. Often we blame ourselves for the state of the relationship, even though we rationally know that we would have remained heartfully connected with them if they had been respectful. We would have found a way, if there was a way. We just would have. What gets lost in the shame shuffle is the fact that some people are truly impossible. Not just difficult, not just requiring healthy boundaries, but impossible to maintain a healthy rapport with. And their impossibility is not lodged in our actions, or choices, or behaviors. It is not a consequence of our imperfections, decisions, or missteps. It is lodged in their own issues and limitations. It is lodged in where they are at. They are simply IMPOSSIBLE. And the sooner we face that, the sooner we can live a life of unlimited possibility.

I wonder what it will take—on an individual and collective level—before we will stop hiding our love away while we are alive. All that vulnerability and longing hidden beneath a bushel of shame and fear. Armor and vulnerability make impossible companions. If there is anyone in your life today that you want to express love to, but you feel afraid and resistant— just share it. Why delay until a day that may never come? Why wait? I want to create a new international holiday: "Hearticulation Day." On this day, we make a collective agreement to allow everyone to express their love to one another with the assurance that we erect no defenses against it. We just surrender and let it in. I am convinced that this one day could radically change this mad world, made mad by ruptured and closed hearts, made mad by love that never got expressed or embodied. We bury so much real love in the graveyards of our consciousness, and it is time—please God(dess) let it be time!—to excavate it and share it freely. We don't need to wait for the Messiah to show us how. We can show each other.

Shaming is not free speech. It's hate speech. Let's stop confusing freedom of expression with the freedom to belittle. They are not the same thing.

You can't be in your vulnerability if you can't express your anger. Both because it clears the debris so you can open your heart again, and because we cannot touch into the deepest parts of our vulnerability without it. Until our inner child knows that we have the capacity to protect his tenderness with ferocity, he will not fully reveal it. She will only open so much, until she knows that we can hold her safe. This is one of the reasons why those who grew up unprotected as children will often keep their hearts closed. They weren't given a healthy template for self-protection. Sometimes we have to forge that template ourselves, in the fires of our own empowerment. The more sturdily we can touch into and express our rightful anger, the more comfortable we will feel embodying and expressing our vulnerability. The more powerful our roar, the more open our core.

It can be so helpful to express our unsaid words, anger, and grief to those who have hurt us. There is no good reason to carry someone else's baggage up the mountain. It weighs us down on a journey that is already challenging enough. Better to shed it so that we can move into life with greater freedom. At the same time, we have to be sure not to make our healing dependent on how others receive our expression. Many of those we share with will be too unconscious, stubborn, or defensive to take in our experience, even if we express it in the gentlest of ways. It may be too shocking to their ways of organizing reality. It may be too painful to face. Not everyone is ready or able to do the deep work that self-reflection demands. This is not to say that we hold back—we must express our truth one way or the other—but it is to say that we are best served by sharing it without expectation. The liberation lies in the expression itself.

You don't measure love in time. You measure love in transformation. Sometimes the longest connections yield very little growth, while the briefest of encounters change everything. The heart doesn't wear a watch—it's timeless. It doesn't care how long you know someone. It doesn't care if you had a 40-year anniversary, if there is no juice in the connection. What the heart cares about is resonance. Resonance that opens it, resonance that enlivens it, resonance that calls it home. And when it finds it, the transformation begins...

Look, it's up to you—it's always up to you. You can deny, repress, distort, and bury your unresolved wounds all you want. You can re-frame them, pseudo-positivity them, detach from them, bypass them. You can re-name yourself, hide away in a monastery, turn your story around. And you can spend all your money on superficial healing practices and hocus-pocus practitioners. But it won't mean a damn thing, if you don't do the deeper work to excavate and heal your primary wounds. The material is still there, right where you left it, subconsciously ruling your life and controlling your choices. This is the nature of unhealed material—it is alive, and one way or the other, it will manifest itself in your lived experience. It will language your inner narrative. It will obstruct your path and limit your possibilities. It lives everywhere that you live. And so you have to decide—excavate it and bring it into consciousness where it can be worked through and integrated; or repress it and watch it rule your life. It's one of the hardest truths we have to face: If we don't deal with our stuff, it deals with us. There is no way around this. Choose.

When we flee our shadow, we flee ourselves. It's not all light in there, of that we can be sure. And that shadow that we fled with all our might, doesn't go away. It waits around the next bend to trip us up and to remind us that it wants to be seen. Not because it wants us to suffer, but because it wants us to heal. Because it wants us to grow. Our shadows aren't the enemy. Our resistance is.

Everywhere I look, I see people who don't want to be here. They don't want to die, exactly, but they don't want to be here. And it's not only apparent in their addictive patterns, its apparent in everyday ways: self-distractive tendencies, shallowing of breath and perspective, perpetual positivity, the transcendence bypass, to name a few. There are billions of ways to leave the moment. I often wonder, what has to happen before we can co-create a world that invites us to be here, truly here? And how can we construct that world if we have already left it? Where is the bridge back to here?

If there is anything that reflects your stage of development spiritually, it's your behavior. You can't call yourself enlightened, if you are a self-serving ass. You are either aligned, or you're not. Enrealment, or enbullshitment—pick your path.

So many of us carry a deep wound around parental neglect or abuse. Some of us carry it so deeply that we are unable to recognize or manifest our magnificence, our reasons for living, the sacred purpose that resides at the core of our being. Intrinsic to these blockages is the core belief that we are unworthy, sourced in our parents' behavior. We carry forward the childhood assumption that their unloving behavior was a reflection of our own value. And this is the gravest of mistakes. Because if someone has a child, and is in a state where they are emotionally and circumstantially capable of loving, their natural impulse is not to neglect or abuse. It is to love. It is to support. It is to protect. If they didn't, it is entirely a reflection of their own challenges, conditioning, circumstances. It doesn't say a thing about your value. In fact, it has nothing to do with you at all. They just couldn't do any better. They were trapped inside their own unresolved issues. They were lost on their own misguided path. Don't let your life's path be a reflection of their limitations. Walk your own way now...

Letting go is hard to do, particularly when the connection has been a true spiritual engagement. It is so complicated when the soul is involved, to imagine letting go... but letting go we must, or perhaps, better to think of it as a kind of letting through. Letting the pain through the holes it leaves behind so it can find its ultimate destination. That doesn't mean you let go of the love, but it may mean that you surrender the dream of being together. Never easy, but sometimes a necessary step on the path to wholeness. Our souls expand when we see a relational adventure through. All the way through to the transformation at their core. To let go is to let grow.

It's one thing to briefly detach from personal story in the hopes of gaining a different perspective—it's quite another to deny our storied roots altogether. What will we stand in, then? At a time when our stories have been shamed and shunned in the spiritual community, it is all the more imperative to revive them and make luminous their sacred, transformative properties. The past is not an illusion, as many would suggest. It is the ground of our being, the karmic field for our soul's transformation, a living vibration that echoes on, the mystery that threads right through our history. Story is where we come from. Story is what roots us in the present. Story is how we arrive at the next place intact. A spirituality without story is like a body without breath. Dead to the world.

It's a different thing, to make a relationship sacred. When it's just the love you honor, you are still in two different worlds. You love her, she loves you, but what stands between you? What of the bridge between your hearts? What of the world you become together? Conscious relationship is all about the third element— the alchemical combination of two souls merging, the living breathing world that you co-create in love's cosmic kiln. It's the difference between loving and serving love. It's the difference between the narcissistic quest for ecstasy and the joys of deep devotion. You serve loving. You are a devotee to the dance. The conscious-nest is a world unto itself.

When you reach a stage where you can have a very dark and difficult experience, without having to look on the "bright side," then you know that you have made progress on your healing journey. Because one significant measure of our emotional health, is our capacity to tolerate all of our experiences without jumping to reactive reframes. You reach a stage where you can stretch to accommodate the truth of your lived experience. You have enough light inside, to own the shadow. And enough shadow inside, to own the light.

Sometimes we are angry at someone who is important to us. And sometimes, we don't get the opportunity to resolve it with them. Perhaps they have faded out of our lives, or perhaps they have passed away. This may trouble us, leaving us feeling guilty or ashamed. But we must remember that sometimes people wanted us to be angry with them. They wanted there to be a rift between us. It's the way that they barricaded themselves against connection. It's the way that they avoided vulnerability. Sometimes the real issue does not lie within the conflict itself, but in the purpose that it served. Sometimes, the conflict was just their way of hiding from love. They wanted you to be angry at them, because that felt easier than being close. Conflict is not always what it seems.

Sometimes the people with the greatest potential often take the longest to find their path because their sensitivity is a double edged sword—it lives at the heart of their brilliance, but it also makes them more susceptible to life's pains. Good thing we aren't being penalized for handing in our purpose late. The soul doesn't know a thing about deadlines.

I always try to remember how much courage it takes for abuse victims to return to a state of trust in this world. This is no game, and often takes every ounce of energy and faith one can muster. Trauma is not simply a concept or an idea of something. It is a deeply embodied experience of suffering that fastens itself tightly to the cellular (and soulular) structure of every person who is victimized. It embeds itself as somatized memory, and it cannot be wished away or bypassed with positive affirmations and victim-bashing mantras. It just can't. I often hear people telling others 'to get on with it,' 'let it go,' and 'stop playing the victim.' This languaging adds insult to injury, and is both counter-productive and patronizing. This is not to suggest we should cling to trauma as our identity, but it is far worse to pretend it isn't there. The heal is for real, and that healing can only happen in a compassionate and patient environment. May we support those who have been traumatized (which is most of humanity, in my estimation) with an exquisite depth of presence and understanding. Trust me, it will serve us all.

When valued personal relationships go silent, trouble often follows. I'm not talking about productive 'time-outs' that are clearly expressed—I'm talking about silence that is reactive, or an attempt to do harm. This kind of silence ensures that the connection will not find its way back to health. Because silence fosters confusion, projections, and worst of all—assumptions about what the other is feeling or thinking. And assumption doesn't get us anywhere good. Inquiry does. Assumptions ensure that the wall will only get thicker, until there is no way to reconnect. Whatever you do, even if you are justifiably angry, try to keep the door to inquiry open. You may not be ready to process the experience, but allow for the possibility that you one day will. Because valued connections are hard to find in this crazy world. Anger doesn't have to be the end of the story. Sometimes it's the portal to a closer connection. Sometimes, it's the way through to great learning. Inquiry is the bridge.

Don't make your healing journey dependent on anyone else's healing. You can't control that. And you can't know whether it would actually serve them to engage in a healing process at this time. Maybe it would, or maybe it would open a pandora's box that would ravage whatever is left of them. Maybe they are keeping it under lock and key for a very good reason—because they do not have the egoic capacity or the emotional bandwidth to work it through. For some of us, it is all we can do to put it away, and go on. Otherwise we may fall apart at the seams. Better to focus on your individual process. Because breaking the generational cycle of wounding doesn't require that our abusers and neglecters own their actions. It requires that we heal from them.

It's important to remember that the coping strategies that helped you to survive, may not help you to heal from what you survived. They were defense mechanisms, parts that you developed in order to manage unbearable realities. They were the best friends many of us had, as children. But healing requires something different. Our healing requires that we peel away the adaptations and disguises and come back to our vulnerable core. Our armored warrior's willfulness, our imaginative defense mechanisms, are now impediments to our quest for transformation. We can't come back to center, if we are identified with those parts that protect it. This is not to say that we harshly sever from what has served us. No, no, we do it slowly, lovingly, gratefully bowing to the best allies we ever had, as they assume a more secondary role in our life. A centered life is not a defenseless life. It's one where we live from a sturdy and integrated core. Our defenses are no longer all that we are. They are places we consciously go now and then, before returning to the magnificent core of our being.

The greatest defeat is not the end of a relationship… it's the unwillingness to learn from it. Most love relationships end, yet the opportunities for growth live on. We have been conditioned to believe that endings are failures, but they are not. At this stage of human development, it's all we can do to manage our own issues, let alone unite happily with another. We still have so much to learn about how to sustain love. The real victory is growing through the experience, clarifying and healing our issues, converting the unresolved material into the transformation at its heart. Relational success is not a tangible outcome—it's a process of awakening. If the experience grew you, if it prepared you for a more heartfelt and awakened life, it was a true victory.

Many people spend their whole lives in waiting-for-validation prison, endlessly trying to gain the approval of others. Often birthed in their dynamics with invalidating parents (who themselves were invalidated), this disempowering pattern is a shame-fulfilling prophecy, one that leads us nowhere. Because even if people validate you, it won't be enough. You will just go looking for it somewhere else. And that won't get you anywhere either, because the issue isn't validation. The issue is the mistaken belief that another human being can liberate you from your self-hatred. They can't. Because they are trapped inside of the same prison. Under-validated people seeking validation from other under-validated people. An impossible cycle. A hopeless waste of energy.

Oh magnificent one, please stop seeking the approval of others. Don't you see? You have already been approved. You have already passed the divine test. You're here, for God's sake! Your validation is within the heart of each breath. Breathe in—I am loved! Breathe out—I am loved… What will it take before we get it?

It is often true that we are projecting our past experiences and relationship dynamics onto others. This is particularly the case where trauma was involved—we can see the abuser, everywhere. But what is also true, is that not everything we see in another is a projection. Sometimes, we have learned a thing or two from our past experiences. Sometimes we have developed a very precise clarity about certain behaviors and intentions. Sometimes we see a similarity that actually exists. So, when someone tells you that you are projecting your difficult mother, or your narcissistic ex, or your impossible employer, take the inquiry to the next level: Am I unfairly projecting, or am I sensing something that I am familiar with? Am I making a misguided assumption, or am I seeing through to the truth? Am I living in the past, or have I simply learned from it?

It's okay to not be ready for love. It's okay to leave, if you can't hold it safe. It's okay to acknowledge that you need to take your focus elsewhere. You have to be true to your own path. You have to go where you will grow. You can't be where you aren't wanting to be. But, one thing... please do it in the way that is most gentle and honoring. Do it in the way that is the most self-admitting. Do it in the way that you would want it done. It's not the leaving of love that shatters hearts. It's the lack of explanation. The lack of accountability. The lack of closure. Leave in the way that you would want to be left—with dignity and a heartfelt respect for the one left behind. Let them know, truthfully and to the best of your understanding, why you have to leave. Speak your truth with courage, even if it hurts. That step alone will transform your inner world. That step alone will support their healing. That step alone will prepare you to love, when the moment is right.

No two wounds are created equal. No two traumas were identical. No two victims experience their suffering the same. It is very important to remember this when we tell others how they should feel, or how they should process their victimhood. What works for one person, or one trauma, may not work for another. And, it has been my experience, that sometimes it's the most sensitive and brilliant among us that take the longest to heal. So, share your healing wisdom, if invited, but never imagine that your answer is theirs. Our gifts are as unique as our sufferings. We each have to find our own path to healing. And the last thing we need to hear is that we are perpetuating our own victimhood when we take our own sweet time.

One of the most reliable indicators of a friendship's longevity is something I call "Imperfection Tolerance." That is, the friendships that are the most likely to last have an expansive and compassionate tolerance for each other's imperfections. Instead of turning away from one another because they are imperfect, they turn toward one another. Instead of shunning each other, they accept each other—warts and all. Quite often, friendships fall apart because there is an inequality in their "Imperfection Tolerance." I have seen this time and time again. One person has little tolerance for their friend's imperfect patterns, while simultaneously expecting all of theirs to be fully embraced. A sense of inequality sets in, as they feel entitled to complete acceptance, while never letting their friend off the hook. Better to identify these patterns early—it will save you lots of time and disappointment. Equality of compassion is the root of most long long-lasting friendships.

Your story is your glory.

You want to live a holy life? Heal your heart.
That's the best meditation of all.

I hear so many spiritual teachers trying to re-frame and put a positive spin on people's suffering, when what people most need is for someone to actually hear their experience deeply. To get in close and really listen. Attuned and empathic listening goes a lot further than telling people that their story is not true, that it was all karmically perfect, that it all happened for a growthful reason, that they chose it so they should be grateful that it manifested. We won't heal the planet that way. Really, we won't. It's time to pass around the talking stick and REALLY listen.

You can't talk about your purpose without talking about your pain. It's tempting to focus only on the light of our callings and offerings—but that's only half the truth. The other half—and in many cases, far more than half—is the relationship between our painful life experiences and the life purposes that they forged. There's a reason why people who had it easier, often find it difficult to find their true-path. Without something to overcome, they lack the resilience necessary to find their purpose in a distractive world. Working through and overcoming our traumas ignites our resilience, and lights a fire of sacred purpose deep within our souls. When we see how hurtful the world can be, we also see the many ways that we can make a difference. In the heart of our suffering, the calling to heal this bloodied planet. Let's get to work.

It's amazing how much energy we can channel into chasing love and approval from those who cannot offer it. It's like our self-concept gets enmeshed with the wrong people—the neglectful ones, the abusive ones, the ones who have yet to move from love. And then the mesh turns into a prison, locking us inside of our own longing, waiting for a liberator that will never come. Because some people cannot love—they just can't. Some people cannot stop taking their misery out on others, locking you in with their unresolved pain. The greatest act of self-love is to let them slip back into their darkness, and to walk towards your own light. It doesn't matter who they are—parents, siblings, partners, colleagues. Let them go. Grant yourself permission to be loved. God or Providence has already stamped you with supreme approval. That you are here is evidence of your inherent value. No need to look for it in those humans who cannot give it. No need to wait on the impossible ones. Begin with those who recognize your value. Begin in the mirror. Stay there until you see what has always been true. There's a lighthouse in your soul, shining bright through your divine countenance. Look close, closer, closest, until you see... You.

Love is the easy part. Relationship is the challenge. But then you knew that. In the old days, they really believed that finding love was the hard part. And then they were startled when they found true love, and things got difficult. But now we are coming to understand that it is often quite the opposite. That working through the unresolved feelings and issues that get in the way of love is the hard part. It is, but there is something quite profound in that, if we can stay together and see the process through. Something happens to our understanding of love. No longer a projected imagining, we come to see it in a far more substantial light. What we once called love was just the beginning. What comes later, after years of watching each other bravely confront the challenges, is the real thing. Where before a flight of fancy, it now has roots... everywhere.

Breaking the cycles of familial dysfunction is no easy thing. Because they are deeply rooted ancestral patterns. Because they are socially acceptable ways of being. Because they are reflected in the systems that frame our reality. And perhaps most significantly— because they are deeply familiar to us, habits that call us home. As the conscious healing revolution picks up steam, we have to be mindful of the role that habit plays in perpetuating our unhealthy patterns. For many of us, home is where the habit is. Even if a behavior has been persistently painful, humans will often continue to engage in it. Because it feels better than the unknown. Because it gives us an odd sense of continuity. Because it connects us energetically to those who came before. Breaking an ancestral cycle requires far more than learning new behaviors. It also requires a courageous willingness to let go of the (dis)comforts of home.

Shaming people for what they "should have known" never supports progress. Helping them to see what they don't yet see, does. It's very easy to look down at those who don't yet see what you see. But where does that get us? Nowhere. There are many things I did, because I didn't know better. And even if there is something I now see, there are also many things I don't yet see. We are all victims—and victors—of context. If you believe in individual and collective transformation, you realize that we are always at a particular point in our development. We see through the eyes of our context, and as that context evolves, so do our *realeyesations*. That process can't happen alone. The road to change is fraught with patterns and potholes. And we need each other to traverse new terrain. We need each other to be our eyes, as we forge new pathways of possibility. Let's do that with compassion. Let's do that with reverence for each other's contribution. We are all seeing each other home.

The whole planet is riddled with misplaced aggression. It's more popular than strawberry cheesecake. People are so overcome with repressed rage, that it simply has to leak out somewhere, often in the direction of innocents. Sometimes it comes through as physical violence, and more often in the form of emotional abuse, passive aggression, scapegoating, and persecution. And none of this will change, until we learn how to process and express emotions from an early age. Until society normalizes the sharing of our woundedness, and imparts techniques for healthy release. Until we learn how easily humans are traumatized, and create conditions that prevent it. We do this, and we change the world. We don't do this, and we are doomed to destroy each other (and our planet). Because all that trauma forces us to repress our memories and dissociate from reality. It compels us to choose paths that are not amenable to healing and wholeness. It turns us into a splintered cacophony of suffering. And in a splintered state, we can't help but do damage to ourselves and others. To break the cycle, we have to get to the roots of our aggression: our unresolved pain and anger. We have to fully own what we are carrying. We have to heal this humanity.

You can't really run away from home. Because you bring it with you everywhere you go. There can definitely be value in escaping to another geography—to protect yourself, to breathe, to get perspective—but you will still have to go back down the path and reclaim your childhood. Because it is still alive in you, still dictating your relational patterns, still controlling your choices. It must be owned. It must be confronted. It must be healed. And until it is, it's still the place you live.

"What doesn't kill you makes you stronger!" Really? Yet another trauma-avoidant survivalist cliché that is intended to keep you looking for the bright side when you are down on the ground, bleeding from a knife wound. Sure, sure, sometimes, your traumas can make you stronger. Kind of like the way that heat hardens steel. And sometimes they can f*ck you up good, destroy your will to live, and debilitate your capacity to trust. When in the presence of someone who was almost killed by trauma, don't remind them of their strength. Remind them of their tenderness. And invite them to be gentle with themselves as they endeavor to heal.

It can be difficult to not take it personally when an abuser or neglecter cannot admit their mistakes, especially if they are people we were close to at one time. But it's not personal. Many abusers simply do not have the egoic strength to face what they have done. Because of whatever traumas they have endured in their own lives, they have never developed the structural foundation necessary to absorb their shame. Without a measure of psychological intactness, it is very difficult for them to acknowledge their fragmented parts. This is not to excuse their behavior, nor to deny its effects, but only to acknowledge that their inability to take responsibility is theirs and theirs alone. It is not something to personalize, to wait for, or to let delay your healing. It's a reflection of their own limitations.

I am seeing a great many individuals teaching work-shops in things they know very little about, and I am seeing many playing with fire (i.e. trendy ayahuasca practitioners) with no training in working with the trauma material that emerges in their sessions. When I began to explore holotropic breathwork, I had been in therapy for years. I still had (and, still have) more healing to do, but I had enough of a foundation to hold myself safe. If you don't have that foundation yet, you may be easily seduced by many of the dissociative practitioners who present themselves as healers. Be extremely cautious, and remember that spiritual healing and yogic soulebrity are now industries, ripe with manipulation and projection. Many who practice in these areas have no regard for your well-being. Be vigilant and surround yourself with those who understand the delicate, and often dangerous, nature of trauma. Trauma work is no game. No transcendence bypassers, no flaky masters, no artificial forgiveness and pseudo-positivity proponents, no 'New Cage' pain-body 'story' bashers, no name-changing Westerners dressed in guru garb. Only solid, integrated, emotionally mature practitioners need apply.

Perhaps the most difficult relational pattern to shift is the tendency to be attracted to unavailable people. Often rooted in the early life unavailability of one or both parents, this stubborn primal pattern can easily obstruct any possibility of partnership. Because if you are only drawn to those who are not drawn to you, you can spend your whole life chasing the impossible. It's kind of like looking for a dance partner in an empty ballroom. You are trying to get the attention of someone who is not actually there. To heal this pattern, it is imperative that you do deep, somatic work around your early experiences. There is something inside you that longs to be healed, and until it is, it will be difficult to take seriously those who take you seriously. It will be difficult to feel an energetic charge toward those who feel one for you. Because they are reflecting back to you something that you have yet to believe—your inherent worth and beauty. You see, they know something that you don't—they know that you are worthy of love. Now you have to do the work to see it, too.

If you have a calling, you have no choice but to humanifest it. If you have a choice, you haven't found your calling yet.

They were allowed to name you, but they weren't allowed to label you. They were allowed to encourage you, but they weren't allowed to shame you. They were allowed to protect you, but they weren't allowed to abuse you. They were allowed to teach you, but they weren't allowed to control you. They were allowed to praise you, but they weren't allowed to define you. They were allowed to hold you, but they weren't allowed to fondle you. They were allowed to support you, but they weren't allowed to abandon you. They were allowed to nourish you, but they weren't allowed to neglect you. They were allowed to birth you, but they weren't allowed to worth you.

Our parents were confused. Often well-intended, but still confused. That's why we have to do all this work to re-parent ourselves. Because they couldn't. That path is ours to walk. That path, our ancestral destiny. We are all doing brave work here. Let's salute each other for our efforts. Pioneers of healing, standing proud. Adventurers in self-creation, crafting life on our own terms.

We have nothing to hide, and nowhere to hide it. It just takes so much energy to bury our truth, and what can we reveal that hasn't been others' experience anyway? Our secrets aren't that unique. They are intrinsically human. Let's practice the arts of radical transparency & shameless self-admission. Imagine truth circles in every community... "I admit..." and then we dance.

It is often difficult to recognize the connection between early-life feelings of imprisonment, and our subsequent need for space and distance in our adult lives. Many can never see that pattern in themselves. And so they run, driven by the illusion that the issue is their job, or their city, or their relationship; when, in fact, it's their unhealed issues that are stoking their flight. For a time, these coping strategies can actually serve a counter-balancing purpose, as our spirits breathe a healthy sigh of relief after years spent entrapped. If your early-life was marked by engulfment, then it is essential that you have a taste of freedom and spaciousness. But, taken too far, these escape hatches can actually become a prison of their own making, one that deepens our isolation and prevents us from forming positive bonds with the world. Any imbalanced reality will ultimately have an imprisoning quality. Just because our early-life environment felt like a prison, doesn't mean that we can't create a different reality—one that is rooted in healthy boundaries and heartfelt connectiveness. The first step is owning our fear of engulfment before it swallows us whole.

Every member of a family is entitled to their perspective, memories, and feelings about their parents. No two children will have had precisely the same experience. Each dynamic is inherently unique. Yet it is often the case that siblings will attempt to pressure other siblings into seeing things the way they do. They will stubbornly push their own ideas of obligation and duty, and sometimes attempt to influence or manipulate perspectives, with no regard for the fact that their siblings may have endured much more trauma with the parent(s) than they have. Factions get formed, people get shunned, and everyone ends up isolated. While the abusive patterns that came through the ancestry are simply perpetuated and preserved. Instead, try a new way of being on for size, one that invites all siblings into a deeper sharing and healing, one that invites inquiry rather than assumption. See the divisions in perspective not as a basis for conflict, but as an opportunity to grow together. Create a space for a mutual empathy process, one where everyone gets heard and seen. This way everyone gets the space to exist, and in ways that they may have been denied as children. Bridges get formed, where before there were needless barriers...

More truthworkers, fewer lightworkers. Because truth is more grounded and inclusive, encompassing of shadow AND light, giving us a much better chance of making a real difference.

We must protect our blessings. Not just the ones that walk through the door to become our friends and lovers, but those blessings that we self-created through our own efforts. We work hard to craft a life that reflects our goals and callings, and one wrong move… one distracted decision… and we can lose it all. Because momentum is a fragile thing in a distractive world. The more aligned your life is with your truest path, the more care-filled you have to be with the choices you make. Protect what you have created with vigilance, while marching forward to the next stages of self-creation. One eye on the prize ahead, one eye focused on the reality before you. This is the path to the life you want.

Polyamory (the path of multiple lovers) is a very popular path nowadays. For a mixed bag of reasons. Sometimes people aren't ready to commit. Sometimes they don't have the space or time to honor a singular connection. Sometimes they need a vaster range of experiences to inform their path. Sometimes they feel imprisoned in one area of their lives, and need freedom in another. Sometimes they are fleeing their issues. And sometimes their sacred purpose is simply not centered around monogamous connection. It's all good, when it's something two lovers happily choose. But if one prefers it, and the other doesn't, it can be a living hell. This is happening more and more, as monogamists are being convinced by their poly lover that there is something lacking in them when they refuse to participate. That they are not open enough, or not 'evolved' enough. For someone who has formed a monogamous attachment, remaining in a polyamorous relationship can actually be traumatizing—taking them deep into jealousy, abandonment, and betrayal wounds that cannot be resolved in this way. If that is you, resist the pressure and come back to your own path, your own truth, your own knowing. There is nothing inherently wrong with either path. The question is—which path is true for you?

I am glad you were born. Such an important thing to say, but so seldom heard. I wonder what would happen on this planet if we said it to each other on a regular basis. Even to seeming strangers we encounter on our daily travels. I am glad you were born—the anti-shame mantra. I am glad you were born. I am glad you were born. I am glad...

Not all traumas were caused by mistakes that require a lesson to avoid repeating them. In fact, most serious traumas weren't mistakes on the part of the victim. They weren't events summoned by their unconscious or their karma, to teach them something they needed to learn. They were victimizations. They were attacks. So, let's stop telling trauma survivors that they must learn a lesson from their experiences. That's just another form of gaslighting. Sometimes there is no lesson. Sometimes, the most they can do is heal. Let's support that.

It is impossible to entirely avoid abrupt endings in our lives. Anything can happen at any time. At the same time, I do believe that we can become better at protecting ourselves from those who have a tendency toward "Abrupt Departure." They are not easy to spot—some reveal it in their agitated energy, their inherent volatility, their perpetual inability to sustain connection. Others are more subtle, quietly held, difficult to read. You have to get to know them a little better before you will see it coming. Once you do, it is essential to self-protect. Not because they necessarily have a malevolent intention—many simply don't know any other way to deal with and communicate their feelings—but because Abrupt Departure is a trauma that is difficult to recover from. If you have been shaken by it—in the form of shocking deaths, or unexplained and unprocessed disconnects—it can be difficult for the nervous system to calm down and feel relationally safe. It can be difficult to trust human kindness and connection. The way back is to practice the art of selective attachment—learning how to distinguish between those who can stay firmly planted in the fire of relatedness, and those who can't. Because we don't want to give up on human contact. We just want to make it safer.

Below the surface of the 'story,' is the real story of our lives. Because we are made of story—there's no shame in that. The illusion is illusion, itself. So, don't discard your entire story. Look below the story to the real story. There is something there waiting to be healed and converted. There is no true identity independent of the story of our lives. We just haven't learned how to read our own storybooks yet. And, once we can read their unique language, we see how they include the soul's codes for our evolution and development. Our wholeness doesn't begin beyond story. It begins within it.

Love can happen in a split second. Bondedness can't. That's the thing we learn the hard way. That love is not the end of the story. It's just the first chapter. The next chapters demand that we acknowledge our wounding, clear our emotional debris, strengthen our capacity for attachment, learn how to authentically relate, mature in the deep within. Chapter after chapter of refining our ability to meet love with a true heart. This is the work of a lifetime. Our opus of opening. How terrifying. How delightful.

May all our relationships be gentle.
We are all trauma survivors.

We are often energetically drawn to those who reflect our childhood wounds and issues. Sometimes we do this in an unconscious effort to heal. But sometimes, we are actually drawn to those who do not reflect our childhood wounds and issues. Sometimes we are drawn to those we have very little energetic charge with because we want to use the relationship as a place to hide. As we become more intimate with the idea that relationship can be a forum for awakening, we need to be on alert for both. That is, is my choice of partner an attempt to heal, or an attempt to hide? Is there enough energetic clay here to grow me forward, or am I delaying my transformation yet again? We should be more afraid of avoiding our path than walking it.

The key is to be realistic about the pace of the healing process. Many of us turn back when things don't change quickly. And yet many of our unhealthy patterns and issues were formed as defenses against feeling difficult emotions. They are ways that we unconsciously protected ourselves from real or imagined harm. They may well have saved our lives. As a result, they have to be processed in manageable increments, and they have to be met with safety at every turn, or they will just harden and intensify. This takes time.

Bottom line—Although your defenses were birthed in harshness, they cannot be healed in harshness. You have to welcome them into your arms, like the tenderling warriors that they are. You have to welcome them home, like victorious soldiers. They came into being in an effort to protect you from harm. Only when they know that you are safe, will they lay down their arms and surrender. If you move too quickly, they go right back to war. A little patience goes a long way.

We die inside when we silence our rightful expressive inheritance. We die inside when we let fear of judgment obscure our knowing. We die inside when we shame and bypass our feelings. We die inside when we choose a path that isn't ours to walk. We die inside when we forget our magnificence, encoded within us from the beginning. I am so tired of the little deaths of self-diminishment. Better to live true.

To live with an open heart is to walk a hero's path. There is nothing more difficult in this armored world, and there is nothing more profound. It's easy to head-trip, to focus, to fixate, to manifest, to detach, to bypass the world of feeling. The world rewards us when we accumulate at the expense of our authenticity. But detachment is a tool—it's not a life. And it all comes at a terrible price, because we cannot be in the moment if our heart is closed. Truth is the gateway to the moment, and we can only know truth through the eyes of the feeling heart. Open wide…

LONGER
HEARTICULATIONS

The humanism bypass. I did it for years. I saw glimpses of someone's potential, their beautiful soul, their loving heart, and told myself that this was who they truly were, ignoring all the rest. But the rest was no illusion—it was them, too. The rest was where they lived most of the time. The rest was what destroyed. This self-destructive pattern was birthed in two places: One, my deep desire to see the best in my difficult parents. Not for them, but for me. I needed to believe that there was something kind and caring living inside of them. Two, a misplaced projection from my own self-concept work. I held the belief in my own potential, as a way of overcoming the shame I carried. But I made the mistake of assuming that everyone else was just as eager to find their light. Of course we all have innate glowing potential. At the core, we are all magnificent beings with profound capacities. But how many of us fully actualize it? At this stage of human development, not so many. The trick is to hold the space for two things at once: a deep belief in everyone's possibilities, and a deep regard for your own well-being. It's okay to pray for everyone's liberation without joining them in prison. Pray from outside the prison walls, while taking exquisite care of yourself. It's okay—you can't do the work for them anyway.

Not everyone will heal in this lifetime. It's important that we accept and understand this. The perpetual emphasis on acknowledging and healing trauma is a beautiful thing, but it's not for everyone. Because some of us don't have the capacity to heal. Some can't even get out of bed, because of the weight of their pain and the complexity of their trauma. Too much has happened, and there is no possibility of transformation. This is very hard to accept in our toxic positivity culture, one where trauma is the new buzz word, and where people forget that they are not walking in someone else's shoes. Just because you were able to heal parts of your past, doesn't mean everyone can heal parts of theirs. We have all lived in a trauma-inducing culture. Some of us didn't make it through in one piece. That's a fact. And if we can just accept this, and honor and comfort them as they are without any effort to 'heal' them, we actually stand a chance of co-creating the kind of trauma-sensitive world that avoids this level of suffering altogether. Because trauma is perpetuated by insensitivity. Our tendency to turn a blind eye to the truth of people's suffering, to shame them for not healing, to blame it on their karma and their choices, is precisely the dissociative consciousness that perpetuates the trauma cycle. Better to accept people right where they are. Better to provide comfort to the fallen ones. That alone will heal the world.

$$\sim\!\!\!\sim$$

Next time you have a terrible thing happen to you and someone says, "You choose your every experience," knock them unconscious. ☺ When they wake up again, ask them to thank you for actualizing their dream. And then, insist that they forgive you before they have even healed their head wound. Then tell them, "Pain is an illusion—just be aware of it, witness it, and you will come into the 'Power of Now.'" Then, remind them that there are no victims and that they just need to "turn around" their story of victimhood. When they try to get up, push them back down on the ground, and remind them, "Everything you see and experience is a reflection of you." Tell them: "You must have had some issues that you needed to look at around violence. I gave you a gift. Be grateful." When they begin to get angry, remind them that anger and judgments are substandard emotions, and that there is never anyone to blame. If this doesn't soften their edges, inform them that the ego is the enemy, and that the part of them that is perceiving this situation as unacceptable—is merely misidentified: "You are trapped in the matrix, and seeing the world through that limited lens." Tell them you are here to liberate them. And then, steal their wallet, and demand they give you their PIN. So they can learn another valuable lesson about attachment and manifestation.

(p.s. Don't actually do this. ☺)

———◦

It is a very confusing time to be a man. I am encouraged to de-armor and soften, but if I open too much, I find myself ill-prepared to manage the workplace and the still edgy elements of society. It is still a survivalist world, after all. And if I don't open at all, I live without real intimacy and I am at risk of all manner of disease— the emotional and physical illnesses that emanate from a closed heart and rigid musculature. So I seek to find a balance, a gradual transformation, recognizing that real change takes real time, and that I cannot transmute my warrior conditioning overnight.

Three things that have helped me to open, while still maintaining my solidity are: (1) Conscious Armoring: That is, learning the difference between an open and armored state, and developing a practice of only putting on my emotional armor when I know it's truly necessary. Not as a matter of habit, but as a matter of necessity. And, remembering to de-armor when I no longer need it. (2) Shedding emotional (and physical) holdings at a measured and humane pace. That is, owning any baggage that I carry, steadily learning the tools I need to release it, and creating space in my life—when realistic—to let some of it go. One release at a time. (3) Trying new ways of being on for size. That is, granting myself permission to expand beyond my habitual ways of moving through the world and within my own body. For example, allowing myself to relate to others with more tenderness, being more receptive in relationships, exploring surrender and self-revealing as a way of being, learning what it's like to not tough my way through life.

Intrinsic to this process is a necessary willingness to confront the internalized shame I experience when I do not respond in typically 'manly' ways to people and situations. Perhaps more than anything—these internalized judgments impede my transformation—because their roots are so very deep in the male psyche. The key is to allow myself to voice the judgments, to return to my traditional ways as often as I need to, before adventuring outward again in a different way. It's going to take centuries to transform the male psyche in a more enheartened direction. One person can only do so much, and, at the same time, every step is significant. When I make a small step in the direction of a new paradigm, I feel like I am carrying a whole crew of ancestors along with me. I can almost hear them breathing a sigh of relief, "Thank you Jeffrey—that armor was damn heavy. It's nice to finally surrender..."

I often hear people say that anger is not the real emotion. That below it is always grief, or sadness, or some other feeling. This is sometimes true, but it's been my experience that it is not always true. Often our primary emotion is anger, and it signals that we have been violated in ways that matter. It's as real as real gets. Imagine yourself as a perfect circle. You are intact. Now, imagine yourself being violated by someone, or by something that happens to you. You become angry. Now you have a choice. You can express it, if possible, thereby preserving the integrity of your being. Your circle is still intact. Or, you can bury it, and watch as it undermines the integrity of your beingness. If there are too many dents in your beingness, it becomes very difficult to function healthily in your life. You end up hobbling through life as a dented circle. The only way to restore your integrity, is to push that dent back out. Not violently, unless self-defense is necessary, but assertively, expressively, with vigor. In other words, you own that you are angry, and you take action to release and express your rightful rage. Anger is a sacred force when it is honored authentically, without needless destruction. It is a legitimate emotion that signals that you have been violated. Don't carry it, bury it, or ferry it from place to place. Express it.

～

Even if we have not had our needs met by our parents for decades, we often go back for more. It is a deep hunger to finally be nurtured, seen, and loved by those who brought us into being. But it has been my experience that those who cannot meet our needs seldom change. Not because they don't want to, but because they just aren't up to the task. They don't have it in them. They are in too much pain themselves. If you are someone who keeps going back for more, you have to stop. You are holding yourself hostage. It's no longer them—it's now you. It's the unconscious hope to finally feel seen and loved that is holding you back. The key to your liberation is to finally see them for who they are. Really see them, the way you want to be seen. See them in their fullest context, their woundedness, their limitations. Once you do, you no longer imagine them as adults capable of meeting your needs. Because they aren't. They're lost children, stumbling over their own patterns and conditioning. They can't meet your needs because nobody ever met theirs.

Of course, reaching this stage of awareness is no easy feat, because you have to achieve this without getting what you needed from them to grow developmentally. It's a kind of catch-22, one that requires that you fully see them as the fractured humans that they are, with no part of you imagining them as intact adults with something to offer you. It's a monumental and difficult step. But it's the only step you can take. And when you take it—I mean, really take it—you become free to get those needs met by those who can actually meet them. You become free to truly live.

There is a time to rescue another, and a time to turn our attention to ourselves. Years ago, I was confronted with a situation with a friend who had spiraled, yet again, into a drug and homelessness trip. It had happened many times before, and I had always put my life on hold to rescue them. This pattern had deep roots in my survivalist family history. This time, I contacted a spiritual teacher—Ram Dass—and he said the one thing that finally broke the back of this pattern: "The most you can do for all of us, is to become all you are meant to become." Both because of his words, and because of where I was at on my path, I was just ready to listen. And, so, for the first time, I stopped the rescue missions and got back to what called me.

Years later, that same person overcame their challenges, and said, and I paraphrase: "There wasn't a thing you could have done for me, until I decided if I wanted to live, or die. You were wasting your time, and actually keeping me from the abyss I needed to confront in order to make that decision." Simply put, some of us don't want to be here, and will inevitably find a way to leave. Others will choose to be here, but not until they are at the very end of their rope. Rescuing may be the right thing in one context, and the thing that enables and perpetuates their suffering in another. Sometimes they need your help, and sometimes they need to be left alone, to face the abyss. Sometimes they have a choice to make. Let them make it.

Praises for the Trauma Speakers—Let them Whisper your Heart Back to Life

I can't possibly know what the most traumatized among us have experienced, nor do I have some simple healing solution that will transform their suffering.

We are only just beginning to understand the nature of trauma on this planet. We are only just beginning to understand that we are all trauma-survivors, to one degree or another. We are only just beginning to listen to the real story of our lives, after generations of denial, victim-bashing, ungrounded attempts to 'rise above' it. But I do know that we need their voice, more than ever, to save this species.

In the survivalist world that we come from, the most traumatized individuals were the most shamed and shunned. It was survival of the 'fittest,' authenticity and healing be damned. If you could punch your way through the pain and accumulate, you were deemed a success. It didn't matter what your inner world or personal life looked like, so long as you championed the material world.

But that way of being is coming to an end. It is no longer serving us. Those in denial around their pain, those focused exclusively on mastery and material achievement, those who imagine themselves 'self-determined' (while negating all who have contributed to their 'success'), are actually destroying our species and the planet that houses us.

We can no longer live in a world that defines success in comparative terms. We can no longer inhabit a reality where our greatest success stories are those who fled their pain the fastest, hiding their unhealed brokenness behind an over-compensatory materialism.

I am not fooled by the egoic accumulators of the world. They are merely lost children, confusing their bottomless quest for worldly validation with healthy self-regard. They will never find peace, in this way. It is a soulless path.

It is time for a world that champions the survival of the truest. That stands down the accumulators and elevates the authenticators.

A world where success is not measured by our ability to out-achieve our neighbor, but by our ability to remain heartfully connected to one another. A world that honors those who have the courage to feel and acknowledge their victimhood, to share their painful stories, to invite all of us to self-reveal. A world that celebrates those who are brave enough to own their uniqueness in the face of judgment and ridicule. This is the only world that can last.

In this next-step world, those who have suffered

the most will be our greatest teachers. It has been so artificial for so long, that we need the trauma-speakers to save us. Because they are the closest to the truth of all of our lives. Because they are the most connected to the feelings that we are all burying—the individual cries for relief, the ancestral unresolveds that thread through each generation.

It may seem counter-intuitive in this conditioned world, but those who have the courage to own their pain, are actually the ones we need the most.

So next time you feel tempted to turn away from someone who wants to share their horribly painful story, stop. Just stop. Ask yourself why you are so eager to go—are they reminding you of something you don't want to feel within yourself?

Then listen closely to them, and let them whisper your heart back to life.

How to Prepare Emotionally for the Death of a Difficult Parent

My Mother passed away a few years ago. I always imagined that there would be more time for us to heal the rifts. I was wrong. She died at seventy-six, in the same harsh way that she lived—dizzily falling to the ground and banging her head, while alone in her apartment. She was a remarkable woman, both in her capacity for overcoming, and in her absolute refusal to be awakened by her challenging life experiences. She fought for her right to live with a tremendous ferocity, and then put all of her energy into self-distraction after claiming victory. If she had channeled the energy that she used to uphold her emotional armor into personal transformation, her awakened consciousness would have lit up the world. She was that powerful.

I did tremendous amounts of therapeutic work on our relationship over the years. I somehow knew that I had to, both because the emotional debris was obstructing my path, and because I didn't want the impossible nature of the connection to haunt me. And yet, despite my most genuine efforts, I fell prey to the most common occurrence after losing a parent: self-blame.

Death gives us new eyes, and sometimes the lens is hazy.

It's always amazing to me how quickly we can forget the reasons that we were not close to someone, after they have died. Suddenly they were saints, suddenly we didn't try enough, suddenly it was all our fault. If only we had called them more, if only we had sent them gifts, if only we had forgiven their actions, if only we had taken them to that one medical specialist that would have saved them from themselves. On and on it goes, yet another opportunity to shame ourselves, as though we alone were responsible for the state of the relationship, as though we alone were the crafters of their pain and misfortune, as though their issues and patterns did not exist before we came into being. It's quite a thing the way that ancestral shame finds a way to perpetuate itself. It's quite a thing.

After she died, I spent the summer inquiring into this inner narrative, paying attention, trying to understand where it comes from within me. The most obvious answer—internalized guilt from a shaming family— didn't quite explain it. I had done enough work around the relationship to know its impossibilities, to know that I had done my best. It had to be something else. And so I stayed with the narrative... and then it dawned on me. My mother is no longer in her body-suit. She has shed her wounds and her baggage. She is no longer emotionally threatening. She is no longer difficult to relate to. She is more vulnerable than I have ever known her. And through these eyes, it's easy to glorify her. It's easy to feel safe with her. She feels saintly, kind, and accessible. She feels like someone I could easily love and connect with. And it is therefore easy to blame myself for 'neglecting' her. After all, she is non-threatening and harmless. She is finally quiet. But it isn't real—not even close. Because when we were both in these body-suits at the same time, a deeply loving relationship wasn't possible. There was too much pain in the way, too many issues and differences. And her armor was still intact, armor that she had developed throughout her life to shield her from emotional risk. In fact, our real-time relationship was a true reflection of its inherent impossibilities. There really was no way in.

It's important to remember this after someone close to us goes, particularly someone we had challenges with. There was a whole world of events, experiences, and choices that led to the state of the relationship. All deeply real. All embedded in our cells as memory. All in the way of healthy connection. As glorious as we may imagine them after they have gone, that was simply not the way they were, when they were struggling down here on Mother Earth. They were human, and so were we.

Until you lose a parent, you are somewhat asleep on the path to awakening. Trust me on this. It's a whole different world after they go. This is true whether you are close to them, or not. The preparation work you do before they go, may be the most important inner work you ever do. Left to its own devices, the shame-game postscript will obstruct and distort a real healing—a healing that is rooted in the reality of the dynamic itself. Better to do real work around this before the parent dies, if there is anything that is unresolved in the dynamic itself. Clearly, there is no perfect preparation—I will continue to work through these issues for years—but there are ways to soften the blows. I offer these suggestions, in the hope that they will be of service to you...

Connecting with the Difficult Parent

If a difficult parent is still alive, and if there is enough safety to bridge to them, do all that you can to connect to, work through, and express anything you are holding. This includes unhealed grief, unexpressed anger, unresolved experiences. Anything that feels incomplete or unsaid. Leave no stone unturned in your efforts to heal and come to terms with the past. If you can bring them into therapy to deepen the process, do so. If not, find any way that is available to you to express what is true for you. Anything that will help you to understand the dynamic and to be liberated from the toxic aspects of the relationship. The focus of this process is not on forgiving them for their actions. It may well happen organically, but the focus here is on healing your own heart and coming to terms with what you have been through. To make sense of the effects that their messaging, availability, and ways of relating may have had on your ways of moving through the world. And, if necessary, forgiving yourself for anything that you mistakenly blame yourself for within the dynamic.

Of particular importance is doing anything possible to humanize your lens on the difficult parent. To see them for who they really are. To walk inside their shoes. Again, you don't do this for their benefit. You do this for yourself, both as a valuable part of healing, and so that you will be less likely to glorify them after they are gone. The more you see them in their humanness now, the less likely you are to forget what you were dealing with later. The more you understand where they come from, the less likely you are to blame yourself for the limitations of the connection. One of the great ironies of our relationships with difficult parents is that they can be held on a kind of primal pedestal, often more elevated than loving parents who gave their children what they needed to individuate and become adults. Through a healthier lens, loved children can often see their parent(s) more clearly. But those of us with a difficult parent are often trapped at an earlier stage in our development, still waiting for the elevated parent to reach down, pick us up, and give us what we need. There is an aloofness and confusion in the dynamic that can keep them forever elevated, and this projection can become a recipe for our own self-abuse after they die. Because we don't accurately perceive them, we carry forward the childhood belief that we must be responsible for all that happened or, at the least, that they would have loved us if we were worthy. To avoid this shame trip, do all that you can to see them for who they really are, while you have the chance, so that you are less likely to up-frame and mischaracterize them later. This includes understanding the context they emerged from, the choices they made with respect to their own path, their patterns with respect to connection and vulnerability, their unactualized dreams and unresolved memories. The bridge from stagnation and self-blame to empowerment and self-love lies in our ability to see the parent(s) for who they really are; to take them off their primal pedestal and recognize their human limitations. This is certainly not easy—the hungry child-self clings to fantasies—but it is so very necessary.

Healing in the Absence of the Difficult Parent

If the difficult parent is not available or open to a healing process, then work on the relationship nonetheless. We don't need a willing counterpart to work through the effects of a connection. If you can afford it, work with a therapist on the many ways that the relationship has landed within you. Clear emotional debris. Become conscious of the connection between their hurtful words and actions and your own issues and beliefs. Work determinedly to shed any internalized negativities, patterns of self-blame, ancestral shame. Confront and fully name the ways in which the dynamic has lived itself out in your daily life. Centuries of survivalist conditioning have made it difficult for many parents to live up to a healthy standard with respect to their children. As a result, many of us are left with a negative imprint of their unconsciousness, carrying it forward often without realizing it. Fully confront and name those imprints, in an effort to liberate yourself from the parental ties that bind. Body-centered psychotherapies are particularly valuable in this work, both because they allow you to connect in more deeply with the repressed emotions, and because they have developed techniques that are effective at moving them.

Talk therapy can be effective, but it can also concretize our issues and challenges if the process becomes too cerebral. Whatever you do, be sure that your therapeutic process supports the excavation and release of the feelings held in the body itself. This will lead to a more thorough, sustainable transformation.

Because the parent is not available for process, it may be more difficult to develop a deeper understanding of who they are and the context they emerge from. To help with this, do all that you can to dialogue with your parent's friends or other family members. Anyone who can help you to understand the pressures they faced, the childhood they experienced, the messages they internalized. Look at old pictures if they are available. Feel into them intimately (you are safe now). Work with them in an effort to clarify your lens. In addition, devote some time to studying the era that they lived in. Keep in mind that a parent's behavior was consistent with their times. Times have since changed. Like us, they were embedded in and influenced by particular ideas of gender, child-rearing, duty and obligation, religious perspective. It can be especially helpful to spend some time watching films, reading old newspapers and magazines, to develop a richer understanding of the limitations and relational patterns of their generation. You don't do this in an effort to excuse their behavior—you do this in an effort to understand their context. Again, the more you can understand where they were coming from in their relationship with you, the less likely you are to personalize the state of the connection. We go back in time, in order to move forward more freely.

Resolution Doesn't Have to Look a Certain Way

Whether you are doing this preparation work in the presence or the absence of the difficult parent, it is important to remember that resolution of the relationship is not always possible or even desired. The bridge between you may be destroyed, or you may be dealing with an impossible person, one who is simply incapable of doing the reflection work necessary to heal the rifts. If the latter is the case, accept this without continuing to come back for more disappointment. I have a cousin who hated his father, but went back every day and sat with him for hours, hoping and waiting to finally get the attention he craved from early life. He never got it, and by looking for it in all the wrong places, actually perpetuated his own stalled development and wasted countless hours of his precious life. Only after his father died did he begin to look for it in those who actually valued him, and to begin the work of learning how to validate himself from the inside out. Until we accept the limitations of those who cannot love us, we cannot embrace the willingness of those who can.

In addition, it is also important to remember that resolution doesn't always look a certain way. Sometimes it is soft and kind. Sometimes it is fierce and erratic. Sometimes accepting the impossibility of the connection is the resolution. And sometimes the resolution is accepting that it was perfect, despite its impossibilities and challenges, because it carries us to the shores of our own empowerment. I think about my relationship with my mother. She was a difficult person, but she gave me great gifts, somehow balancing the just-right tension between worthy adversary and protective mother. For many years, I bought into the idea that we had to find our way to a perpetual peace, that our ultimate resolution had to be smooth and tender. But why is that? Why must resolution look a certain way? Perhaps the connection was exactly as it was meant to be, in order to bring me through to this awareness, this form of expression, this balance of vigilance and tenderness. Perhaps she gave me the exact gift she came to bring, and that is the resolution right there. Perhaps...

However we look at it, it is clear that the more deeply we can work through the material around the relationship, the less likely it is that we will beat ourselves up after the difficult parent is gone. The more likely we will be able to grieve our loss healthily, without obstructing our own process. And, in this way, we break the cycle of shame and abuse that has carried forward from one generation to the next. We set the stage for a new way of being. We heal humanity forward. And perhaps we heal it backwards, as well. With every clearing of our emotional debris, with every foray into a kinder way of being, we heal the collective heart. So many of our familial and karmic ancestors had little opportunity to heal their pains. They just towed them along, not realizing that there was any other way. When we heal, their spirits surely breathe a sigh of relief. We heal them backwards, while healing ourselves forward. Mending the ancestral ties of time. We heal in unison. That healing begins in the trenches of our own transformation.

3 Tools for Building
a Healthy Sense of Self

After a traumatic and disempowering childhood, much of my life's work has been about building a healthy and empowered sense of self.

Not a narcissistic sense of self, but one that is rooted in a healthy ego and a recognition of the great possibilities that live within each of us. I believe that every one of us comes into this life with a brilliant and unique sacred purpose, a network of gifts, callings, lessons, significant relationships, and key emotional issues that we are here to clarify, to express, to actualize, and to grow through.

Our sacred purpose is our unique contribution to the world.

In order to fully embrace our purpose and make self-affirming life choices, we need an authentic sense of our own value. We need to believe that we are worthy of bringing our gifts and offerings to the world. Because so few of us were given a healthy template for self-validation, we often have to forge that template ourselves, in the fires of our own determination.

Here are three tools that helped me reach the stage of self-validation where I could see my purpose through in a challenging world:

TOOL 1
Practice the Art of Selective Attachment

Given that our sense of self was wounded in relationship, some part of it has to be restored through relationship. We are relational beings, after all. But relational healing can't happen with just anyone. We have to cultivate the art of selective attachment.

In other words, we have to sift everything through a self-validation filter, connecting only to those relationships that support our healthy self-development. If someone bolsters our sense of value, we invite them in. If they don't, we turn them away. In other words, self-validators enter, lite-dimmers exit. Not from a place of contempt, but from a place of burgeoning self-love.

We already have enough internalized voices telling us that we don't have value. We don't need any more. If they don't help you grow, then let them go. Who you surround yourself with really matters.

Of course, we can get all the validation we want, even if it comes from someone credible, but it won't be enough. We still have to take proactive steps to confirm our value.

TOOL 2
Affirm your value

Affirmations can be a positive step in the direction of self-empowerment. It can be encouraging to repeat self-validating affirmations throughout the day. For example, "I am enough," "I am worthy of a healthy relationship," "I am worthy of self-love," "I am brilliant." These mantras can keep you going, particularly during challenging moments, and can bolster your sense of self.

On their own, they are not enough to deeply transform you. In order to build a strong and sturdy sense of self, your words need to be coupled with self-affirming actions. In other words, you need to prove to yourself that you matter. You have to make your affirmations real. There has to be a congruency between what you are expressing and what you are living before your inner world will take notice.

By making your affirmations real, you send a message to the deep within that you are worthy enough to wage this battle for self-love. If we don't prove to ourselves that we are willing to fight for our right to the light, and our right to a healthy self-concept, who will?

This work may require that we go to the edge of our discomfort, and make empowering new choices. For example, if you are someone who has had a hard time speaking up for yourself, shift the pattern by clearly and confidently voicing your needs or desires. Or if you are someone who has resisted exploring a more gratifying career path, take one step in the direction of a new career.

Even the smallest and shakiest of steps can transform your inner landscape.

To make your affirmations real, finish the things you start. Prove to yourself that you can see things through to completion. This can include both important and meaningful life goals, or practical and menial everyday tasks. It doesn't matter if they are lofty accomplishments or simple actions. What matters is that you drown your negative self-talk in a sea of accomplishment.

TOOL 3
Heal Your Core Wounds

Fundamental to our efforts to self-validate is the importance of going back into the past to heal our core wounds. At the heart of a diminished self-concept is invariably some combination of unresolved abuse, trauma, and unmet needs. And it's seldom ours alone. Most of these dysfunctional patterns have roots in our family lineage and ancestral patterns.

In other words, we are carrying everyone's emotional material up the rocky mountain with us.

The way we break free from dysfunctional familial patterns is not by running away from them. It's by walking back in their direction. Not because we want to keep repeating them, but because the only way to shift these patterns is to heal them at their roots. It's okay to run from them for a time, but not for all time, because the flight from what lives inside of you merely delays your arrival.

You may think you are on the way to a new destination, yet the plane keeps circling back to your childhood home. It can't navigate a new flight plan until you return back to where you came from and heal your broken wings. With your wings strengthened, there is nowhere you can't go.

The healing can happen in many forms. Talk therapy can be an effective tool in seeing and understanding the roots of our diminished sense of self. With the right therapist, you can talk through and reclaim those parts of yourself that got lost along the way. You can come to terms with where the voices of self-hatred and internalized shame originated.

But identifying and analyzing our wounds is not always the same as healing them. Excessive analysis perpetuates emotional paralysis, strengthening our mental capacities while possibly delaying our deeper healing. An effective recipe for healing is to couple your talk therapy with a body-centered psychotherapeutic approach. Body-centered models like Somatic Experiencing, Bioenergetics, and Core Energetics engage both your mental faculties and your capacity for deep feeling, supporting a more integrated healing. Your negative self-talk may be manifest as thinking, but its roots are often in the traumas endured within the emotional and physical bodies.

Our traumas were a felt experience, and if we want to transform them we have to meet them directly, within the body itself. The feel is for real.

The key to the transformation of challenging patterns and wounds is to heal them from the inside out. Not to analyze them, not to watch them like an astronomer staring at a faraway planet through a telescope, but to jump right into the heart of them, encouraging their expression and release, stitching them into new possibilities with the thread of love.

You want to live a self-empowered life? Heal your heart. That's the best affirmation of all.

About the Author

Jeff Brown is a breakthrough voice in the self-help/ spirituality field, and the author of six popular books: *Soulshaping: A Journey of Self-Creation, Ascending with Both Feet on the Ground, Love It Forward, An Uncommon Bond, Spiritual Graffiti,* and *Grounded Spirituality.*

In his previous life, Jeff was a criminal lawyer and psychotherapist. Since pursuing his path as a writer, he has launched many initiatives, including founding *Enrealment Press,* and an online school, *Soulshaping Institute.* He is the producer and key journeyer of the award-winning spiritual documentary, *Karmageddon,* which also stars Ram Dass, Seane Corn, Deva Premal and Miten. He has written a series of inspirations for ABC's

Good Morning America and appeared on over 300 radio shows. He also authored the viral blog 'Apologies to the Divine Feminine (from a warrior in transition).'

A popular presence in social media, Jeff's new terms and well-loved quotes became a phenomenon some years ago, and continue to be shared by millions of seekers and growers worldwide. His quotes have been shared in social media by *Brain Games* host Jason Silva, actress Chrissy Metz, songstresses Fergie, Alanis Morissette and LeAnn Rimes, and many others. Most beautifully, they have touched and benefitted millions of souls.

In the spring of 2018, Jeff was invited to Ottawa by Sophie Gregoire Trudeau—Gender Equality Activist— and the wife of Canadian Prime Minister Justin Trudeau. A dear friend had passed his books to Sophie some years prior, and she began sharing quotes from Jeff's work in social media. They began to exchange ideas about many mutually resonant themes. After sharing some of his writings in speeches and dialogues, she invited him to the nation's capital to film a conversation with her about emotional healing and gender equality. Here is a link to excerpts from that conversation:

https://www.facebook.com/SophieGregoireTrudeau/videos/2039199436332994/

Jeff now understands that each step on his path laid down the foundation of a new model: Grounded Spirituality. The challenges he faced, and the countless steps of overcoming were intended for this purpose: to support humanity in their efforts to embody all that they are. Not to bypass their humanness, but to celebrate it. Not to find enlightenment independent of the self, but to find enrealment deep within it. Here we are, just as we are.

Jeff currently lives in Canada with his wife, poet Susan Frybort. He is presently breaking new ground as an Enrealment Activist, with lots of exciting plans in the works including: a facilitators' training course for Grounded Spirituality; a soon-to-be-launched podcast and video interface; a plethora of new courses at Soulshaping Institute; co-creating benevolent movements; traveling the world teaching and connecting with his supporters.... and whatever other unexpected surprises await this wildly rich path of Sacred Purpose. You can connect with his offerings at jeffbrown.co, soulshapinginstitute.com, karmageddonthemovie.com, and enrealment.com.